the secret life of money
A KID'S GUIDE TO CA$H

KIRA VERMOND
Illustrated by CLAYTON HANMER

Owlkids Books Inc.
10 Lower Spadina Avenue, Suite 400, Toronto, Ontario M5V 2Z2
www.owlkids.com

Distributed in Canada by University of Toronto Press
5201 Dufferin Street, Toronto, Ontario M3H 5T8

Distributed in the United States by Publishers Group West
1700 Fourth Street, Berkeley, California 94710

Library and Archives Canada Cataloguing in Publication

Vermond, Kira
    The secret life of money : a kid's guide to cash / by Kira Vermond
; illustrated by Clayton Hanmer.

Includes index.
Issued also in electronic format.
ISBN 978-1-926973-19-7 (bound).--ISBN 978-1-926973-18-0 (pbk.)

    1. Money--Juvenile literature. 2. Finance, Personal--Juvenile
literature. 3. Children--Finance, Personal--Juvenile literature.
I. Hanmer, Clayton, 1978- II. Title.

HG221.5.V47 2012   j332.4   C2011-905814-6
Library of Congress Control Number: 2011935956

Canadian Patrimoine
Heritage canadien

Canadä

Ontario
Ontario Media Development
Corporation

Canada Council Conseil des Arts
for the Arts   du Canada

ONTARIO ARTS COUNCIL
CONSEIL DES ARTS DE L'ONTARIO

Société de développement
de l'industrie des médias
de l'Ontario

We acknowledge the financial support of the Canada Council for the Arts,
the Ontario Arts Council, the Government of Canada through the Canada
Book Fund (CBF) and the Government of Ontario through the Ontario Media
Development Corporation's Book Initiative for our publishing activities.

Manufactured by Printplus Limited
Manufactured in Shenzhen, China, in October 2011
Job #J1109012

A   B   C   D   E   F

Publisher of Chirp, chickaDEE and OWL
www.owlkids.com

Dedication and thanks

For my crackerjack sounding board, who gave me tons of ideas and even drew me pictures: James, Jay, Max, Michael, Charlie, Emerson, Maren, Taryn, and sweetie-pie Elizabeth. Kate and Scott from Central Public School, thanks for lending me your library. Speaking of which, Amanda, you're way too cool for school. Tristan, thanks for pitching in on a yuck Saturday and getting me out of a pinch. This book is also for Nadia, Dayle, and Dave, who gave me time in the summer to write it. Stand up and take a bow because I'm so gigantically grateful. And of course, Nathan, who read it and laughed at all the right places. I didn't even have to pay you (much).

Kira Vermond

CONTENTS

CONTENTS

"*Money will buy you a pretty good dog, but it won't buy the wag of his tail.*"

– HENRY WHEELER SHAW

People
like you

THE
BEGINNING

What's pie got to do with it?

MONEY. IT'S A LOT LIKE AN APPLE PIE. Seriously. I'm not making it up. (Okay, maybe I am a little...)

A pie starts with a bunch of random ingredients: flour, shortening, eggs, sugar, cinnamon, butter, and apples. But then you throw them together in a super-precise way, stick the whole lot in a hot oven, give it some time...and voilà! It's just you, a fork, and a half-empty pie plate.

Money's like that, too. A single nickel in your pocket doesn't have much of an impact on your life. Neither does a dime, a quarter, or even a

1

dollar. But once you start mixing all those dollars and cents together—plus a bunch of other people and their funds—suddenly money really becomes something you can sink your teeth into.

People and Pie

- If they get their hands on a pie, some people will polish the whole thing off.
- Others will eat a tiny sliver and save the rest for later.
- Some feel guilty after they eat even one little slice of that luscious apple goodness. (Not me! Bring it.)
- Others demand more pie... even when they've had enough.

People and Money

- If they get their hands on a big wad of cash, some people will immediately run to the mall and spend the lot.
- Others will spend a tiny amount and save the rest for later.
- Some people feel guilty when they spend even a tiny fraction of their paycheck.
- Others want more and more money...even when they have enough.

See what I mean?

That's why I've developed a taste for money over the years. Cash is complicated, but in a seriously fascinating way. It makes us happy, sad, fearful, and even embarrassed. It's got the power to destroy

WHEN IT COMES TO CASH, WE'RE NOT EXACTLY AT A LOSS FOR WORDS

Money, moolah, cheddar, currency, coins, dollars, notes, pounds, dough, greenbacks, bucks, bread, bacon, beans, clams, boffo, loonies, spondulicks. (Spondulicks? As in, "Hey, take these here spondulicks down to the corner store and pick up some milk"? Seriously?)

whole countries and save lives all around the world. Don't say that's not amazing.

Like many of you, I've been interested in money since I was a kid babysitting and selling hotdogs at the hockey arena. What was this mysterious stuff that gave me the ability to buy a new T-shirt or hang out at the movie theater with my friends? And even weirder, why didn't the grown-ups around me ever seem to want to talk about it? These were big questions that needed big answers.

And it turns out I was right. Researching and writing this book has made me realize how mind-blowing money truly is. In fact, I've learned so much this year that even I'm spending and saving my money in a whole new way. (For example, money does buy happiness…if you spend it the right way. More on that later.)

I have to admit I wish someone had handed me a book like this when I was a kid. But lucky for you, more and more people are coming to realize that financial literacy (that's fancy for "money education") is something everyone should have access to a lot earlier in life. More kids are finally learning about debt, saving, and spending in school instead of stumbling across the information when they're adults (adults who may already be in serious debt, because no one taught them how to handle their money in the first place!).

Ready to get started and sink your teeth into money now? Whether you already know how to read the stock markets or you're starting from scratch, this book is going to give you the goods to see money in a whole new way. The payoff is going to be huge. So why not read on?

Easy as pie. That's how money is going to seem to you soon. So flip the page. I'll be waiting for you on the other side.

Kira

"Money frees you from doing things you dislike. Since I dislike doing nearly everything, money is handy."

– GROUCHO MARX

CHAPTER ONE

HELLO, CASH-O-RAMA

What's this book all about?
Oh, yeah. Money. That stuff.

CHEDDAR. BUCKS. MOOLAH. FUNDS. BREAD. BACON. BEANS.
Whatever you want to call your money, there's a good chance you're starting to take it a bit more seriously these days. Maybe you're thinking about taking a babysitting class or mowing the neighbor's lawn to turn your spare time into pure moneymaking magic. Sounds like a plan.

Or perhaps you've already got a wad of cash stuffed in your old piggy bank...and now your mom is telling you it's time to open a real bank account.

And that's where the problems start. Because as soon as a bank gets involved, money can become kind of...confusing.

You start to hear stories about interest and debt, credit cards and loans. Then there's all that weird stuff in the paper about stocks, bonds, taxes, and bull markets. (You're pretty sure that last one isn't about cows at the grocery stores, but still...) And what the heck is a mortgage?

I mean, c'mon. Do you really need to worry about this stuff now?

You're not alone in feeling weird about it. Talking about money can make people really uncomfortable. If you don't know what words like "stocks" and "debt" mean, they quickly seem like a big jumbled mess of terms. Plus, money has the power to make us worry because lots of us never seem to have enough of it. We think that if we have more, life will be better. The result? People will try all sorts of things to get their hands on more money.

Sometimes it works for them. But sometimes it doesn't.

Winners don't always win

Take lotteries. You'd think that if you won a big chunk of change—to the tune of $30 million—your life would be set, right? Your family could buy a spiffy new car, a mansion with a pool, and even pony up for a pony. That's what a lot of people assume. More money = better life.

But that's not always how the story ends. It turns out a lot of lottery winners end up losing all their winnings, and even declare bankruptcy when the cash runs out. Some winners blow *all* their money on boats, cars, vacations, houses, and parties, while others give too much of their winnings away to friends and family and don't keep enough for themselves. Others forget they have to pay taxes on their loot, and before they know it, the taxman shows up and takes any leftover cash. Oops.

Lottery winners' good luck can quickly go bad in another way: Winners get lonely. Imagine your family just struck it big and suddenly you have more money than anyone else you know. At first it feels like a dream come true. But hold on! How many kids in your class will be jealous of you? How many will stop being your friend? How many other kids who barely said hello to you before the win now want to be your best friend? Whom do you trust?

Lottery winner. No free lunch.

Guess what? My friend Deb's family won a cool $3 million playing the lottery. I asked her what she hated most about having the cash. "Nobody buys me lunch anymore. A lot of my friends expect me to pay for everyone's meal!"

Gulp.

Money. You mean the world to us.

Lotteries are a super example of how much power money has over us. That's because **money is never just money**. In other words, cash has a serious impact—both good and bad—on, well, everything.

Money is more than a piece of paper or a coin stuffed into the pocket of your backpack. Think about it—your money decides whether you live in a swanky mansion or a tin-roof shack. It gives you the means to store fresh apples in your fridge, bread on the counter, and soup in the pantry...or merely a bag of rice in the corner of the room. Money influences what bike you ride, whether you go to camp, and even how you feel about yourself. Your parents possibly even talked about whether they had enough money to start a family (read: you)!

Money brings up big, big questions that are really interesting to answer.

Questions like: "Anyone want to make me a millionaire?"

Wanted: A million dollars

In November 2010, a comedian in New York City named Craig Rowin created a video for YouTube that asked somebody—anybody—to give him $1 million. He didn't really want it for any cause, and it's not like he did something specific to deserve it. But wouldn't it be cool if a millionaire or billionaire stepped up and offered to give him the dough? That's what he thought, too.

It was a kooky enough idea to draw in nearly half a million viewers. Even more tuned in for his follow-up video.

Today, Craig insists it was all just a joke, but when he realized the million bucks wasn't coming, he decided to take the gag one step further. He made a fake voicemail message from a mystery "millionaire" named Benjamin, who claimed he wanted to make Craig super wealthy. Then Craig printed off a fake notarized letter so the deal would look more legit.

That's when the whole situation started to travel to crazyville. A reporter for a New York newspaper got into Craig's apartment building and started asking him questions. Was the story real? Was it fake? Was he really going to get a million bucks from a stranger? Then other television and radio stations in the U.S. and Canada started calling wanting to know the same thing. Craig was in a bind.

"I didn't want to ruin the joke and say, 'You're right. You're an investigative reporter. Please ruin this for everybody,'" he says now.

Finally unable to take the pressure anymore, he decided to come clean sooner than planned. He hosted the fake-check hand-off at a local theater and stood up in front of a 170-person sold-out crowd.

"Sometimes you ask for a million dollars and get it, and sometimes you ask for a million dollars and don't," he said that night...before setting the check on fire and revealing the hoax.

A few months later, he says he's still unsure what he learned from the whole experience. He does know, however, that people either loved him or hated him for asking for the million. Because people think of money as having value, it makes us uncomfortable if it's devalued by giving it away for nothing. Especially a sum that big. A million dollars is supposed to mean something, right?

Even Craig admits he would have felt incredibly uneasy if a big shot had actually turned up and given him the money.

"I believe in the goodness of people, but if someone is willing to give you a million dollars for nothing, there's absolutely something wrong with that person," he says.

Money for nothing?

As Craig learned pretty quickly, no one is going to walk up and give us a wad of cash just because we ask for it. No way! If you want money, you usually have to figure out a way to earn it. You sell your prized lizard tank for $50 or spend a day baking bread in a bakery in exchange for a little, well, dough. That's how money exchanges hands in the real world.

Besides, asking for a handout can feel a bit unsettling if you don't know where the money comes from. Craig says now he would have handed back the check if someone gave him a real one for $1 million. Who knows what strings would have been attached to the gift? Would he eventually have had to give it back? Would the money have turned into a disaster, just as it has for so many unlucky lottery winners?

Getting comfy with cash

OK, let's recap...

Winning the lottery? Bad. Asking for free money? Big mistake.

Soooo...what *is* the secret to making money, then? Knowledge. Straight up, the more you learn about cash, the less nervous you feel about it. I've got proof, too.

When I was a kid, there was a big recession and lots of people lost their jobs, including my dad. My parents didn't always have enough cash even to buy me a birthday present. At one point, we ate food donated by a charity. I worried that my feet were growing too big for my shoes. How was I going to get to school without something on my feet? Honestly, that was a big anxiety that would keep me up at night.

But then I grew up and went to university. And I learned about money. Soon, I started making enough money to buy myself a bunch of new shoes, if I wanted to spend it that way. (I didn't! I actually hate buying shoes.)

Above all, I gave money my respect. It deserves it. And as a result—whether times are fat or lean—I feel more comfortable with money. Talking about it. Saving it. Spending it. The whole deal. And that's a much better feeling than worrying about being broke.

So what do you think? Are you ready to become more comfortable with that bread, bacon, beans, bucks, or whatever you want to call that cash in your pocket? Turn the page and let's get started...

"*The mint makes it first,
it is up to you to make it last.*"

– EVAN ESAR

CHAPTER TWO

IT'S
PAYBACK
TIME

Who needs money? We all do!

YOU WALK BY A STORE and look...there they are! A pair of shoes that you've been wanting for months. They're in your size and your favorite color, too. Bingo! All that's left to do is grab them, right? But who's that angry dude in the security outfit coming after you yelling "Stop!"? Oh, yeah. That money thing. You've got to *pay* for those shoes.

You see, as nice as it would be, we can't just walk into a store and take whatever catches our attention. We need to give the shopkeeper something in return.

We use money to pay up because it has value. As a tool for trade, it's worth something. So those bills, pounds, pesos, and francs are mighty useful when you want to buy or sell goods like cars, computers, or cosmetics. They're also used to buy and sell services at home and around the globe, which helps other people buy and sell their goods and services, too.

For instance, if you bought those shoes you wanted, the store would make a profit. If the store makes a profit, the manager can hire more salespeople. If more salespeople sell more shoes, the person who cobbles together the shoes makes more money, too. When enough people have money to buy things, the whole economy improves. When the economy improves, more people feel like buying things, and on it goes…

So money does make the world go round and round, both at home and on the other side of the planet.

Still, money has negative power, too. When it doesn't work, people lose their jobs, many don't have the money to pay for things they need to survive, and sometimes entire countries go to war over it. So money is useful to us only if we can use it to buy things and we can trade it without getting into fights over it or hurting other people out of greed.

It's all about money, honey!

"Hey man, will you pass me that pig? I want to use it to buy myself a new skateboard."

And "money" is…?

Money—usually defined as anything that can be used to make a payment—must be:

- durable enough to last
- hard to counterfeit or fake
- scarce, but not too scarce
- portable
- easy to divide up
- valuable
- accepted by people as the way to pay for stuff

Huh? Believe it or not, everything from salt, shells, feathers, animals, and even 12-foot stones has been used as currency in the past. And even though these items didn't look like our money today, many of them did the same job. That's because they possessed a few important characteristics that all successful money needs.

Have all of these traits, or at least most of them, and what do you get? Money, money, money!

But that's not all it is. Many financial experts say that money is actually more like a nifty and useful *idea*. They say it is an *agreement* between people in an economy.

Weird, huh? At first I was confused, too, but look at it this way: If you and six friends wanted to trade comic books at recess, the comics would actually be your currency. That's because you all got together and decided they were worth something. A country makes a similar decision about money when nearly all its citizens *agree* that a dollar has value.

But now let's imagine that everybody decides a dollar is worthless. It would soon become worthless—even though the coin hasn't physically changed since yesterday.

Why do we need money anyway?

Here's an experiment to try with your friends: Go to you room and gather up all the clothes, toys, and knickknacks you no longer want and throw them into bags. Ask your friends to do the same thing. Then all of you can get together and trade. Hello, "new" video game and excellent "new" jeans.

People have been trading—also known as bartering—since the day Cave Guy wanted to swap his piece of leg meat for Cave Dude's more succulent slab of belly meat. And bartering is still going strong today. Think about it. You've probably bartered at school, trading stickers, colorful rubber bands, and music.

But there's a problem with bartering.

Wanna trade?

No thanks!

RAD!

AWESOME

Bartering only works when both people have something the other wants. This is not a big deal if you're merely trading toys or a snack at school. But it is a major concern if you're trying to trade your wares for, say, food, warm clothing, or other items you need for survival. (And no, your friend's stack of chocolate chip cookies doesn't count.)

So money is a superior way to trade for a very good reason: *everybody* wants it.

Making dough to buy doughnuts

Now that you know why money rules, have you ever looked at a quarter and wondered how that piece of cold, hard cash was created so it would be cold and hard? A country's mint—that's who actually makes the money (for instance, the United States Mint or the Royal Canadian

Mint)—strikes coins between two dies to make the patterns that tell us how much the coin is worth.

Paper money, however, relies on a special offset printing press that gives it colors and lines. Then another press uses tons of pressure per square inch to press the ink into the paper and give it a raised texture that's hard to copy.

At least, that's how countries' banks have been making their paper money for decades. But times are a-changing, and technology is chugging right along with it. Here's what I mean...

Will that be paper or plastic?

Imagine you're a five-dollar bill crammed into a pocket in a pair of jeans. Admit it, things have been a tad boring since your owner chucked his pants into a heap on the floor two days ago. But what's this? Someone just picked up the load of laundry and is now hoisting you down the stairs to the—gasp—washer and dryer!

You know what's coming next. Going through the wash with all that soapy wiggling and jiggling is *not* going to be pretty.

Too bad you don't live in Australia, New Zealand, Vietnam, Zambia, Indonesia, Mexico, or any of the other dozens of countries that use currency made from polymers—plastic money. (By the time you read this, Canada will be on the plastic-banknote bandwagon, too.)

Plastic bills actually make a lot of sense for countries with warm, humid, or wet climates that tend to break paper money down. But slick, waxy polymer banknotes? Not only do they absorb a smaller amount of dirt and grime, but they're less likely to grow nasty bacteria that can make you sick. (Seriously, if you had any idea how many people pick their noses before handling their cash, you'd never touch the stuff again!)

What's that smell?

Sorry to break it to you, but if your hands reek metallic after handling coins, it's not the dirty pennies' fault. It's yours. German scientists have discovered that the smell is actually human body odor, created by the breakdown of oils in skin after touching objects that contain certain metals. And just to jack up the *eww* factor, the same stink occurs when iron-rich blood meets skin. No wonder some people swear that blood smells like pennies.

Small change throughout the ages

A (SUPER) SHORT HISTORY OF SOME WACKY CASH.

Most of us can recognize money today. But would you know it if you saw it in the past? As far as we can tell, this money concept didn't simply start in one place and then travel around to other communities. Instead, lots of different people from many different cultures all seemed to come up with the idea at generally the same time. It seems common cents were just, well, common sense. Here are a few kooky currencies that caught on around the world.

COWRIE SHELLS
7000 B.C.-1900 A.D.
Want those comfy sandals? Time to shell out…
Smooth and with a scalloped edge, cowrie shells were widely accepted as currency all over Asia, Africa, and the Pacific Islands. Even Native Americans used shell money at one time. The most valuable shells? Those used inland away from the sea.

What it bought: Cowrie value was all over the map, literally. But in 1850 in Congo, 10 cowries could be traded for a chicken.

SILVER DENARII
2ND CENTURY B.C.
When in Rome, do as the Romans did—pay with hard-earned denarii.
Unfortunately, a lot of dishonest folks didn't actually want to work for the silver coins, which were used until the fall of the Roman Empire in the 3rd century A.D. Instead, counterfeiters used baked clay molds then washed the bogus tender in silver.

What it bought: A Roman soldier could expect to make a 225 denarii salary for one year.

COCOA BEANS
1200-1521
Beans, beans, the lucrative fruit…
Powerful Aztecs didn't merely use cocoa beans to make delish cups of hot chocolate. Most people wanted them to buy and sell things at the market. The Aztecs were the original bean counters, by the way. They couldn't actually grow cocoa beans on their lands, so they made the tribes they conquered hand them over as tax. The only drawback? Their sweet investment (the beans) would eventually go bad. Rotten luck!

What it bought: A rabbit for dinner in 1513.

WAMPUM BEADS
1500S-1700S
Leave it to the new guy to turn our nice gesture into money.
Traditionally, the Iroquois and their neighbors traded a string of wampum beads as a sign of good faith after a deal was done. But then European ships arrived in northeastern North America. The new settlers encouraged wampum beads to take on new value—as currency—and they were used for buying and selling.

What it bought: In 1657, two strings of wampum beads could buy a fine beaver skin.

PLAYING CARD CASH
1685-1763

Talk about gambling away your fortune.

In 1685, coins were scarce in New France (now the Canadian province of Quebec). Faced with a mob of angry soldiers, Intendant Jacques de Meulles did what any creative (read: desperate) leader would do—he took ordinary playing cards, wrote a value number on them, and had powerful people give them their stamp of approval. Instant money! To make it clear that fakes were a big no-no, Meulles sentenced one counterfeiter to have his hands tied behind his back... for three years.

What it bought: Anything you needed, until the fall of New France to the British. Then the cards were practically worthless.

SHINPLASTER
1775-1783

Shoes too big? Use Shinplaster™ and treat those tender toes today!

Sadly, some money isn't worth the paper it's printed on. That's what soldiers discovered during the American Revolution when paper money the Continental Congress issued became practically worthless. So worthless, in fact, that the troops stuffed it into their stockings for extra warmth.

What it bought: A couple of extra hours before frostbite set in.

KISSI PENNIES
1900-1940

And now for something completely different.

Without a doubt, Kissi pennies are unlike the coins most of us know. Rather than round, the money, used in Sierra Leone, Liberia, and Guinea in West Africa, were twisted iron rods, about the length of a ruler. They were generally used to make small purchases. It was believed every rod had a soul. Break or melt down the rod for its useful iron and...Poof! Good-bye value, hello guilt.

What it bought: You'd have to pay 600 Kissi pennies to buy a cow in 1918.

U.S. BANK NOTES
1914

This dollar has been brought to you by the Bank of New York City!

Until the U.S. Congress put the Federal Reserve in charge of issuing official notes, thousands of U.S. banks were allowed to print and issue their own cash! Today, you can still buy stuff with the newfangled Federal Reserve notes, the only currency still being manufactured by the Bureau of Engraving and Printing.

What it bought: Your full money's worth, that's what. (The value of the dollar started dropping after 1914 and was worth a measly 62 cents in 1929, when the Great Depression hit.)

BILINGUAL BANK NOTES
1935

English or French? French or English? Why not both?

Money was in a muddle when the Bank of Canada formed in 1935. It wanted to eliminate the practice of different banks and even businesses printing their own bills. Good idea, but weirdly, the new official bank issued separate French and English versions that first year. Since then, all Canadian bank notes have been bilingual.

What it bought: Smack dab in the middle of the Great Depression, you could snag a hockey sweater for two bucks. (Today, they can start at over $100!)

Fighting forgers of funds

The plastic variety of money is gaining currency over the traditional cotton- or paper-based options for another important reason: it's harder to counterfeit. Many of the existing plastic bills boast little clear windows or swirls that are tough to imitate. Sure, polymer notes cost more to produce, but according to the Bank of Canada, they're recyclable and last two to three times longer. That means the bank will print fewer of them in the end.

Your mom is right—much of the world's money doesn't grow on trees—and now you know why.

Speaking of printing on polymer, it's a high-tech business. You've got to melt plastic chips, gather the polymer they create into rolls of even thickness, and run them through a press, adding lots of layers of white ink. Small transparent spaces are left to dot the sheets and a laser burns an image into them. It's kind of like a hologram, which makes the bills really almost impossible to scan or photocopy. The rolls are cut into sheets before layers upon layers of ink are applied to give the bills texture. Slap on some serial numbers and they're good to go.

A change for change

So, for a lot of countries around the world, paper money is going the way of the Dodo, while plastic money is riding a wave of popularity. Change is good, right? Not so fast. Some nations are not always willing to embrace anything but traditional dollars and cents.

Take the United States. As far back as 1971, the government has tried to release new dollar coins into circulation to replace the paper dollars. And why not? We know that coins last about 30 years, while paper money hits the shredder after approximately four years. Then there's something called "seigniorage," or the profit made when the feds make the coins for about 30 cents each but sell them to the public for a dollar. By minting dollar coins, the government would save, well, a mint.

Sounds reasonable. But many American citizens refuse to use these shiny, newfangled bucks. They say they're too heavy and inconvenient. Some vending machines won't accept them either.

So here's what's happening: In 2011, it was reported that over $1 billion of the new coins has been quietly building up in the Federal

Meet an Expert!

Manuel Parreira
Bank of Canada

When Manuel moved to Canada from Portugal as a kid, little did he know that some day he'd be burning money—and someone would pay him to do it!

But that's exactly what happened when he took a job with the Bank of Canada, the nation's central bank, about 30 years ago. Back then, when bills were too old or tattered to be used anymore, the other banks would gather the unfit notes up in bags, send them to the Bank of Canada, and Manuel would check that the bags contained what they were supposed to—loads of cash. Once they counted the money, employees would hoist it into a big furnace and burn it up. (Gives new meaning to the phrase "burning through money," doesn't it?)

"After working at the Bank of Canada for a while, money just becomes colored paper," Manuel admits. "You do get used to just throwing it into an incinerator, but at first it's strange."

Since the 1980s, the bank has turned to shredding banknotes instead, something Manuel learned how to do when they stopped printing thousand-dollar bills in 2000. His job? Throwing hundreds of thousands of dollars into the jaws of death.

Today, he's traded in that position to represent the bank. He works with retailers, the police, other banks, and even talks to kids about money and how to stop counterfeiters who make fake bills.

"I'm the eyes, ears, and voice of the bank. The neatest thing about my job is that it provides instant gratification. I can go out and see a difference," he says.

DON'T LET THIS DEAL FLY BY

Looking to unload a little extra cash—say, over $7 million? Then you too could be the proud owner of the world's most expensive coin ever to be sold: the American 1933 gold double eagle. Although 445,000 of these coins were minted that year, President Roosevelt, the U.S. president during the Great Depression, decided wasting all that valuable gold on coins was a great big blooper. The solution? Smelt 'em down! Only a few escaped the inferno, and in 2002, one was sold for $6.6 million (plus a pesky 15 percent buyer's fee). That's what we call paying a mint!

Reserve vaults—because no one will use them! And this mountain of money is expected to grow, since the government created a congressional mandate (kind of like an order) to make more.

Hmmm. Letting a billion dollars just sit in a heap. Kind of crazy, isn't it? That money is enough to buy 284,900,285 hamburgers, or the world's largest private yacht, the *Eclipse* (complete with two helicopter pads, eleven guest cabins, two swimming pools, and a bunch of hot tubs).

Dollar coins? They're not funny money. Use 'em right and they turn into fun money.

Want to find out why jobs like Manuel's pay more than working behind an ice cream counter? Hit the next chapter with me and I'll give you the scoop.

> *"A nickel ain't worth
> a dime anymore."*
>
> – YOGI BERRA

CHAPTER THREE

IT'S OFF TO
WORK WE GO
The value of a day's work...decoded!

POP QUIZ: You get visited by a genie—that's right, the smoky guy from inside the bottle. What are your three wishes?

To be the fastest runner alive? (Eat my dust, Usain Bolt!)

World peace? (Oh, how noble of you!)

Hey, here's a thought: How about an enchanted bag that would spew out cash whenever you wanted it? It's a nice thought...or is it?

Why working works

Since genies don't exist, most of us have got to earn our money the old-fashioned (and magic-free) way. By working. Yes, at a job.

But going to work is about more than just spending your time doing something you'd rather not be doing. Because here's the thing: The jobs that people work at every day do matter. Police officers keep you safe and stop the bad guys. Librarians quickly help you find the books and information you need to write tomorrow's report. (Shhh! I won't tell anyone you've been procrastinating.) A science professor at a university makes amazing new discoveries through research.

8 out of 10
That's how many people say they would choose to keep working even if they inherited enough money to live comfortably. Clearly we work for a lot of emotional reasons—not just to pay for stuff.

Plus, they get paid. And where does that money go? To tips for restaurant waiters, fees for dog groomers, bills from electricity companies that employ other people, and taxes that pay for roads and parks.

So work and money are important for creating a society that we all want to be a part of.

What's more, if we didn't work and everyone quit, that functioning society would change drastically. The world's economies—not to mention public services, stores, and more—would tank. No police? Hello, crime. No science researchers, no new discoveries. And no money to pay for anything.

Will work for food (seriously)

Besides, there's another good reason to keep going to work. According to economist and author Dan Ariely in the U.S., studies suggest that people actually want to work because they identify with their job, not the money itself. Their work becomes a big part of who they are and gives them a sense of purpose and enjoyment. It's one of the reasons little kids, when asked, will tell you, "I want to be a firefighter when I grow up," instead of, "I want to make $45,000 a year fighting fires when I grow up." The job is more important than the money.

Even animals feel the need to roll up their furry little sleeves and get down to business, says Ariely. In one study conducted by an animal psychologist back in the 1960s, a bunch of lab rats showed that they preferred to earn their food instead of going for the freebie.

How? A scientist guy gave his hungry rodent friends easy access to food from a cup—but only after they learned how to feed themselves from a dispenser that shot out a food pellet every time they pressed a tiny bar. Out of 200 rats, only one lazy specimen decided to keep chomping away out of the free cup. The other 199 eventually went back to the dispenser to press the bar and "work" for their food. In fact, some of them rarely ever went back to the free, plentiful vittles.

Animals aside, each person's individual job is worth *something* to society. Each job has value. But how much? Now that's the big question.

What job is worth what?

Ever wonder why a bank president makes more—as in, waaay more—money than your teacher? Or why the person who sells you buttered popcorn at the movie theater makes a lot less than an accountant? How do we decide that some jobs are worth more than others?

Yappa-dappa-doo

Before we answer that question, take a moment to consider the yap stone. Yap-stone money was a currency used in the 1800s by people who lived on Yap Island, found in Micronesia. The stones were made out of aragonite, which the Yap-ites (for lack of a better name) carved into huge, doughnut-like shapes.

Problem was, you couldn't actually find aragonite on Yap Island. Instead, a burly bunch would brave the high seas in a homemade boat to travel to another island, quarry the stones—some as large as 12 feet—and somehow get them back home. The work was exhausting and dangerous.

It was that extra effort and danger that gave yap stones their high value. (You can say similar things about other precious stuff, like gold, which people have to work long and hard to find.)

So...Yap. Work. What's the connection again?

Here's the deal. Just as we give *things*—like the yap stones—extra value because they're hard to make or obtain, we also give people's *time* value, especially if what that person does with it is dangerous, challenging, or rare. In other words, not many people have the skills or talents to do what that person does.

TRICKY
Computer Programmer
$64,000

RISKY
Firefighter
$45,000

RARE
Pro baseball player
$2,632,655

Right, so the more "special" your skills are, the better you get paid at your job. Sound fair? Well, it's a little more complex than that.

So a major league sports player with rare talent makes over 58 times more than a firefighter? Does that makes sense? On one hand, when a firefighter runs into a burning building, she's not only there to save lives, but is risking her own life as well. Some would argue this job is worth more to society than that of someone who plays ball for a living.

On the other hand, very few people can accurately pitch a ball that clocks in at 97 miles an hour (never mind doing that 100 times in a night). And don't forget the massive amounts of money fans fork over to watch each game, not to mention the profits generated by ball caps, T-shirts, posters, and other merchandise. In part, ballplayers make mega moolah because they get a share of the team owner's mega-mega moolah.

Whichever way you cut it, gauging work's worth isn't easy or even logical.

Some professions pay more for another reason: The person who does the job received a lot of training in order to do it right. That training probably took years to complete and cost a lot of money, too.

A hematologist (a doctor who treats blood cancers like leukemia), for instance, might spend more than 20 years in school and fork over hundreds of thousands of dollars to pay for it. Not too many people would become doctors if in the end the job didn't offer enough money to pay off their education! Doctors, of course, also help people and save lives, so that adds to the value of what they do.

So why do bankers laugh all the way to the bank?

That's a question a lot of people started asking in 2008, when the world faced the worst financial disaster since the Great Depression in 1929. Keep in mind here, we're not talking about the friendly teller standing across the counter from you at your local bank. She had no hand in this. But many top bank employees were very responsible for the recession in 2008, by coming up with ways to give loans to people who normally wouldn't receive them. These were people who didn't have jobs, or had a track record of late payment. In short, their credit scores were too low. But some of the big financial bosses decided it would be a good idea to give them the loans and mortgages anyway. Why? They could charge a big fee called interest. The result? A ton of people couldn't pay the loans back (surprise!) and got into a whole lot of financial hot water.

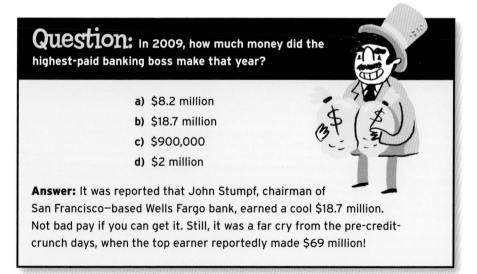

Question: In 2009, how much money did the highest-paid banking boss make that year?

a) $8.2 million
b) $18.7 million
c) $900,000
d) $2 million

Answer: It was reported that John Stumpf, chairman of San Francisco–based Wells Fargo bank, earned a cool $18.7 million. Not bad pay if you can get it. Still, it was a far cry from the pre-credit-crunch days, when the top earner reportedly made $69 million!

Who's worth more? Hospital workers or accountants?

That's what a British think tank organization called the New Economics Foundation decided to find out. It's an interesting question, except that, as you've just been reading, deciding a job's worth can get pretty difficult.

Is one job better than another because it means a big paycheck? Is a job awesome because it involves something fun, like kicking a soccer ball around in front of screaming fans? Or is a job's value best seen through the lens of the good it does for society?

Well, that's how these economists wanted to analyze a job's worth, so they set about answering the following question: "Does our salary reflect how much good our work does for other people and the environment?"

And here's what they came up with:

BIG-TIME BANKERS
(people who move money around to make more money)

ADVERTISING MANAGERS
(people who make the ads that convince us we need a nicer car or cooler clothes)

X Waste $17 of value for every dollar they earn because they persuade us to spend money we might not have. Soon, everyone is irritable.

X Waste $11 of value for every dollar they earn because of the damage they cause to the global economy.

TAX ACCOUNTANTS
(bean counters who help customers find ways to hold on to money at tax time)

X Waste $72 of value for every dollar they earn, if their job is to find ways for people to avoid paying tax. The researchers claimed that if we all just paid up, your town, city, or country would be in much better shape.

"Does our salary reflect how much good our work does for other people and the environment?"

WASTE RECYCLING WORKERS

(they'll take your old plastics, glass, and paper and turn them into things we can use again)

✅ **Create $18 of value** for every dollar they earn by helping to turn old bottles into new bottles, tires into roads, and newsprint into toilet paper.

HOSPITAL CLEANERS

(they clean the rooms and keep germs from germinating)

✅ **Create $15 of value** for every dollar they earn and keep patients from picking up nasty bacteria and viruses that will cause them to get sicker.

CHILDCARE WORKERS

(like your old daycare teachers and babysitters)

✅ **Create $14 of value** for every dollar they earn, since they offer a valuable service for families.

Does this make sense?

Without a doubt, these economists have come up with a new way to look at the issue. I mean, they sure made me think.

But like everything attached to economics, the buck doesn't end here. Maybe high-end bankers deserve a higher salary than childcare workers because they spent years in school learning complicated math. Or because they lend money to people who otherwise wouldn't be able to buy a home without saving up for 20 years first. That's got to be worth something, right? Or maybe daycare workers are paid less because families would have a hard time paying their babysitter $38 an hour if they make only $19 an hour themselves.

Besides, not every accountant is out to rob the government, and not every banker is rubbing her hands whenever people go into debt. Life just isn't that black and white. But here's what we do know for sure: Every job definitely has an impact on other people and the planet. Sometimes good, sometimes bad, usually a bit of both. That's why a job's worth is so hard to pin down by asking if it's good for society. There's usually no clear-cut answer.

Despite all that, some of the employees who made these decisions kept raking in millions of dollars in salaries and bonuses, while other people—maybe even your family or someone you know—lost their jobs and houses.

Even more ironically, some studies suggest that even in financially stable times, the hyper-inflated salaries the bankers receive do more harm than good. They actually make people less productive because that big, fat salary is so distracting. (Hey, how easy would it be for you to concentrate on your homework when you'd rather be thinking up cool ways to spend your *$50,000* weekly allowance?)

History plays a part, too

Sometimes, the history of a certain job tells society how much it's worth—even if it doesn't make much sense anymore. Take book authors and publishers. Back in the day, the only people who had the time to do something as *frivolous* as writing were those who were already wealthy. Publishing was considered a "gentleman's profession." In fact, it would have been quite unseemly to ask for a big advance on a book or demand a high salary as an editor.

Even though that reality is no longer the case for people who write, edit, and publish books and magazines (meaning that they are not just rich people looking for something to do), the industry still pays relatively little for all the work involved.

The blame game is kinda lame

So here's an idea. Let's say we started paying better salaries for more "valuable" jobs. Would you rather be a banker or someone who comes up with nifty ways to make green energy? Would you look at banking and decide that work is not only uncool but also destructive?

Before you make that decision, maybe there a few other factors to consider. Remember, this is only one way to look at how to determine a job's worth. You could also say that bankers do a lot of good, too. For instance, how many families would be able to afford a home without taking out a loan in the form of a mortgage? Not many at all. But banks, and the people who work for them, lend people money for many worthwhile reasons.

Meanwhile, students who might not otherwise go to college or university receive loans from banks to pay for their education. Then fast-forward 10 years. Eventually they find a good job, pay for their kids to go to school, and even give to charity.

Looking at the numbers on the previous pages, it would be easy to label banking careers as incredibly damaging to society, but the reality is far from crystal clear.

It's a complicated business, this business of looking at what businesses we get into.

Money is time and time is money

Bzzz! It's that pesky alarm clock again, telling Future You it's time to get dressed, grab your wallet or purse, and head out the door for work. But are you slipping into a fast-food restaurant uniform or reaching for a briefcase? Depending on your job, not only do your clothing and accessories change, but so does your paycheck. And make no mistake about it, the amount of money you pull in each week has a big impact on how you live the rest of your life. Pay matters.

The poor pay more

Earning less will cost you, and not just in time you'd rather be spending on the beach or digging into a great book. It turns out the more broke you are, the more you'll probably spend on essentials—things all of us buy every day.

- Let's say your dad's job doesn't pay enough money to buy a car, or he's too broke to take the bus or subway. He would probably walk down the street to the convenience store to buy your groceries. And that $1.99 loaf of bread at the megastore could set him back $3.49 at the local corner store.

- Don't have the money for a clothes washer and dryer at home? It's off to the laundromat to spend three hours waiting for the clothes to take a spin. That's time well wasted.

- Credit cards can really hike up the price if you're one of the, say, 37 million people in the U.S. who lives below the poverty line. (That's more than Canada's *entire population*, by the way.) Credit card companies often give people with low incomes cards with higher interest rates, so in the end they'll pay more for their purchase than someone with a better job and a lower rate. (We'll go into interest rates in the next chapter. Stay tuned!)

The poor pay more...

Devin makes $7.25 an hour working at a restaurant as a busboy. Devin has to work...

20.7 hours to pay for a $150 iPod

5.8 hours to pay for a $42 pair of jeans

3.2 hours to pay $23 for a movie and snacks at the theater

53.8 hours to pay $390 for the end-of-year class trip to Washington, D.C.

Josephina makes $10.25 **working for her local drug store. Josephina has to work...**

14.6 hours   to pay for a $150 iPod

4.1 hours   to pay for a $42 pair of jeans

2.2 hours   to pay $23 for a movie and snacks at the theater

38 hours   to pay $390 for the end-of-year class trip to Washington, D.C.

Calder makes $21.50 **an hour working part time at the post office. Calder has to work...**

7 hours   to pay for a $150 iPod

1.9 hours   to pay for a $42 pair of jeans

1.1 hours   to pay $23 for a movie and snacks at the theater

18.1 hours   to pay $390 for the end-of-year class trip to Washington, D.C.

Let's break it down

Earning less money an hour is a big drag—on your personal time. That's because minimum-wage earners have to work more hours to make the same amount as Mr. Moneybags.

At first, the difference between Devin's and Josephina's wages doesn't seem like that big of a deal. What's three bucks? But as soon as you start adding up the hours, it quickly becomes apparent that class-trip-bound Josephina is 15.8 hours richer than her buddy Devin. Plus, she was able to use that time to study, practice with the school choir, and hang out with her friends. And Calder? By landing a well-paying job, he's the hands-down wealth winner.

Money. It ain't what it used to be.

You're hanging out with your grandfather, just shooting the breeze, when he gets started on his favorite topic: money.

"I remember when I could buy a soda at a ball game for 5¢," he tells you. "And if I wanted to ride the subway to the game, that cost a nickel, too."

So what makes that soda at the stadium set us back $3.50 today? Part of the explanation can be boiled down to one word: inflation. Of course, prices go up for other reasons, too. For instance, the price of fresh lettuce can increase by a dollar or more if a hungry swarm of grasshoppers stop in for a bite. Lettuce is suddenly hard to come by, so the price goes up. But when it comes to steady and prolonged increases, inflation is usually the culprit.

Everybody needs to be concerned with inflation because it can affect how much buying power you have. Because even if you do make a good salary, inflation can make the money you earn worth a lot less eventually.

Buh-bye, baby boomers

"You got the job!" exclaims your new boss as he thwacks you on the back and shakes your hand. "In fact, take two jobs! Or how about three?"

Is this some kind of weird alternate universe where job hunters rule the world with their magic powers of persuasion? No, it's the job market of 2021! That's about the time that some economists predict the greatest number of baby boomers—that huge group of people born between 1946 and 1964—will retire. Just in time for you to swoop in and land the job they're leaving behind.

For love *and* money?

Darned inflation. If the price of a bowl of noodles, a haircut, or a skateboard will keep increasing anyway, what's the point of working unless it brings in a load of cash? Hold on. There's yet another way to give a job value—and that's what the job is worth to you.

As the rat experiment at the beginning of this chapter showed us, working to earn money can be rewarding. And if you actually enjoy the work itself, all the better. Think about your favorite subject at school. Is it math? Writing? Science? Now consider how you feel when you're dividing numbers, writing an awesome story, or conducting a cool experiment. That's exactly how it feels when you're doing a job you love. Work feels like play. Oh yeah, and your paycheck pays for stuff, too.

Many people will choose to work a job that pays less than others if it means that they are doing work they love.

No yearnings for earnings

That's right. Not everybody thinks money and high-paying jobs are the answer. Just this afternoon a friend let me in on a secret about her grandfather and his stance on salary. In short, he didn't care much about money. Or rather, he cared about it a lot more than the rest of us.

Gotta get more school?

By 2020, 70 percent of all new jobs will expect you to have some kind of university degree, college diploma, or apprenticeship training.

Jane's grandpa used to turn down raises and high salaries in exchange for lower ones. In one case, a company offered him $3,000 to do a job. He told the new boss he would take it, on one condition: they had to give him $2,000 instead. He decided his profession paid more than the work was actually worth. Besides, he had so much fun doing his job, it gave him more satisfaction than money could buy.

For the record, although my friend respected her grandfather's decision, she still wished he could have just given her the money instead! Because who knows? Maybe she could have used that money to start her own snake-charming business…

Want to start *your* own business (snake-charming or otherwise)? Check out the next chapter.

KIRA EXPLAINS: Inflation!

HOW INFLATION HAS THE POWER TO CRANK UP PRICES AND MAKE THE VALUE OF A DOLLAR FALL.

"If my mom makes $52,000 a year, why does she say she can't afford to buy me a new bike? Where does all that money go?"

Meet your parents. They have pretty good jobs and a nice home. And there's you, itching for a new bike.

Your parents pay their bills on time and even save some of their money when they can. Hello, new bike, right?

Not so fast! Introducing the latest comic episode of "INFLATION! WHAT GOES UP GOES UP AGAIN!"

Even when your folks are doing everything right, inflation comes along and cranks up the price of everything. Why? How?

Inflation crops up when there's too much money. How? Sometimes a country prints extra cash to stimulate the economy (more money = more people buying stuff = more jobs).

Now people have lots of money, but that can pose problems, too. People are willing to buy more things (and pay more for them). With less stuff to go around, businesses raise prices.

Inflation tends to average about 3 percent each year. Something that cost $10 last year will cost $10.30 today.

Inflation is not a big deal when your parents get a raise at work and make an extra 3 percent, too. But if their salaries stay the same... you'll all feel the pinch.

Combine inflation, taxes, and cost of living, and there's not much left over for a bike. But hey! Save cash by making Mom dinner instead of ordering out. Or why not spring for a more economical pogo stick? They're super-keen!

> *"I don't pay good wages*
> *because I have a lot of money;*
> *I have a lot of money because*
> *I pay good wages."*
>
> – ROBERT BOSCH

CHAPTER FOUR

BE YOUR OWN
BOSS, BABY!

Turn that cookie dough business into dough in your pocket.

STRETCH. YAAAAWN! Time to get out of bed and start the day. But what's this? You have no bed, mattress, pillows, or even blankets on the floor. In fact, say good-bye to your breakfast plates, milk glasses, and the laptop you check in the morning to find out if it's going to be a snow day. And your car and bike in the garage? Even they've disappeared, too.

Yep. You've just stepped into the No Entrepreneur Zone.

> HELLO. MY NAME IS...
> *Entrepreneur*
> A person who organizes, operates, and takes on the risk for a business venture.

Dreams build jobs

Think about all the people who ever said to themselves, "Hey, I think I'll start a bed company," or "A business that builds microwaves? Why don't I give it a whirl?" Those people are entrepreneurs. Now imagine what our world would be like if they'd decided to give up on their dreams.

Well, what *would* happen if we lived in a world without entrepreneurs? Not only would our standard of living be a lot less than it is now (seriously, do you want to drink from the river with your cupped hands because no one makes tumblers?), but there would be hardly any jobs. And since entrepreneurs are the ones who take risks on exciting and innovative new businesses, there would also be a lot fewer *interesting* new jobs.

But before you go around thinking that entrepreneurs are just bigwig moneybags who can afford to start up any business they like, think again. In fact, most entrepreneurs are a lot more modest (and younger) than you might guess. An example...?

He's been an entrepreneur since he was seven years old...

That would be Cameron Herold, founder of Backpocket COO, a company in Vancouver, Canada, that helps other entrepreneurs learn how to make a buck. Cameron, to put it mildly, is pretty passionate about people who own businesses. And he believes that lots of kids should think about running their own, too. Not tomorrow, but today.

"Every single company out there—every business, every restaurant, every gas station—one person started it. Someone like you said, 'I want to start this company.' Why not you?" he says.

He should know. Cameron's been cooking up moneymaking schemes since he was just seven. That's the year he started roaming the neighborhood collecting people's unwanted coat hangers and selling them back to the dry cleaner for two cents apiece. Soon he'd collected thousands of them.

Speech! Speech!

"You don't have to have a boss. You can be the boss. If you like to be in charge, if you like to lead, if you like to march to your own drum and do what you want, then do it! Then get other people to follow you."

– Cameron

42

Not only did Cameron make some money, but the dry cleaner got what he wanted, too: coat hangers. Everyone was a winner.

"I'd tell my mom I was going out to play—then I'd just go door to door on another street," says Cameron.

That little coat hanger business was just the beginning. By the time Cameron hit high school, he'd found all kinds of ways to make money without getting a real job. He...

1. Had a paper route, but hired other kids to deliver the papers.

2. Took orders for soda from seniors and delivered it for their weekly bridge games.

3. Cut lawns.

4. Spent one summer at the cottage buying and selling used comics.

5. Collected and sold wayward golf balls he found at a golf course. (Other kids stuck to finding them in shrubs and around the fence. Cameron went the extra mile and fished them out of the pond...with his feet.)

Anatomy of a capitalist

Cameron's the first to admit he struggled in school (he's since been diagnosed with ADHD) and remembers teachers telling him he had to focus. Instead, he doodled and dreamed up new business ideas. Now looking back, Cameron says a lot of the following traits have actually helped him be successful today. He:

- visualizes all the steps in a process starting from the end and working backwards.
- notices business opportunities everywhere!
- leads other students.
- can sell an idea. (He once got in trouble for convincing a bunch of his friends to strip down to their underwear and run around the school—in February.)
- can speak in public with ease. In school he won the citywide speaking competition. Today he's given speeches in seventeen different countries.

Good fortune for fortune

A lot of great entrepreneurs are the first to admit that luck—that's right, LUCK—has a lot to do with their success. It's about being in the right place at the right time.

Does money buy happiness?

It can. But according to one British study, money only truly makes us happy if it makes us feel richer than our neighbors or friends. For example, imagine your teacher is handing tests back and you see you've pulled off an A+. Pretty good! But what would happen if you found out everybody in the class got an A+, too? Suddenly, that awesome mark doesn't make you feel quite as happy.

Now, psychologists (people who use research to tackle real-world problems) have long noted that money does make us happier if it lifts us out of poverty. That makes sense. No one wants to be poor. But if you're part of the middle class (enough money to pay for food, housing, and extras, but not considered rich) it seems you've got to have more than someone else to feel good, claims Chris Boyce, the lead researcher from the University of Warwick.

"Earning a million pounds a year appears to be not enough to make you happy if you know your friends all earn 2 million a year," he said.

Just ask the telephone research guys back in the 1970s who tried to convince us to use their newfangled Picturephone. In other words, you could see the person you were talking to on the phone over a television-like set. Only one problem: No one wanted to yakety-yak in their housecoat or while unshaven in the morning. They just weren't ready for it yet. But now? A lot of us think nothing of pressing a button on our smartphones or other techie devices and getting that face-to-face time with friends and family. Same idea, but right place, right time. (And better picture quality, too.)

Looking for a free ride

Still, all the great ideas, confident planning, and even good luck doesn't change the fact that at the heart of every successful new business lies one thing: hard work, and lots of it.

Work, schmerk, you say? Even the thought of running your own business doesn't excite you? Instead, you dream about winning the lottery or stumbling on some other get-rich-quick scheme? Well, keep dreaming. Money for nothing is often nothing more than a great big hill of trouble. Hop on to these so-called free rides and have a look for yourself. Just remember to hold on tight...it gets a bit bumpy.

FREE RIDE #1: **STEALING!**

What, this doesn't look real?

It's reported that a thief in California was once arrested for trying to hold up a bank branch without a weapon. He used a thumb and a finger to imitate a gun, but unfortunately he forgot to keep his hand in his pocket. The police eventually found him sitting in the shrubs outside the bank and arrested him. No bang...and no bucks.

Thems the breaks...

A group of robbers who stole a cash machine in Australia watched their haul catch fire after they dragged the machine out of the building with a truck and a chain. They sped away with it dragging behind, but the friction caused the machine and the money inside to catch fire. Bet they're burning with shame now.

FREE RIDE #2: **COUNTERFEIT!**

But I didn't know...

A woman who tried to use a fake $1 million bill to buy $1,675 worth of merchandise at Walmart told police it was all just a misunderstanding. Turns out the wonky bill was a gag gift. (The United States Treasury doesn't make $1 million bills, just so you know.)

Not so funny money...

If you suspect you've got a fake bill in your pocket, take it to the police. Don't try to pass it along to someone else and make it their problem. That's a crime. The Criminal Code of Canada, for example, states that anyone caught making, possessing, or passing counterfeit money could receive a prison term of up to 14 years!

FREE RIDE #3: **LOTTERY!**

I'm going to win...

Sure you are. Even if you're feeling lucky, the odds of you winning the lottery are next to nil. In fact, you're more likely to be struck by lightning than win the big one. Want proof? A lottery that asks you to pick seven numbers between one and 69 gives you a one in 1,078,897,248 chance

of winning. (Yes, that's over a billion to one.) By way of comparison, someone eating an oyster has the relatively sunny odds of one in 12,000 of finding a pearl nestled inside. So set aside that ticket-buying money and save it instead.

But if I just buy more tickets...

Yes, spending more money on more tickets will up your chances. If you buy two tickets, you're twice as likely to win, right? Absolutely. But here's the catch: If the chances of winning are one in 1,265,756,641, buying a second ticket will give you only a *two* in 1,265,756,641 chance. Not exactly stellar odds.

FREE RIDE #4: **SCAMS!**

For Pete's sake, just pay the man...

Instead of fighting invading Vikings, some English kings of old preferred to pay up instead. These payments were called *Danegeld* (meaning "Dane debt"). Becoming used to the steady flow of cash, the Vikings imposed a similar tax in Ireland—and slit the noses of anyone who wouldn't or couldn't pay. Now you know where the phrase "paying through the nose" (paying too much for something) comes from.

Meet an Expert!
Teang Tang
Mingle Event Management, Canada

From the time she was about eight or nine years old, Teang Tang knew she was going to run her own business one day.

"I was the kind of kid who wanted to set up a lemonade stand all the time," says Teang, now in her twenties and living in Calgary, Alberta. "Being an entrepreneur has always been in my blood."

Today, Teang owns and operates Mingle Event Management, a company that helps plan special events for businesses, and even weddings and birthday parties. But here's the thing—she likes to plan events that are eco-friendly. Sometimes that means setting up hybrid taxis for people to take home or hiring a chef for a wedding who serves only organic food grown by a local farmer. The idea is catching on. Teang has over 800 customers and hires up to 70 people to pull off the work.

Even more amazingly, Teang built the business while going to university full time! Although she admits things can get busy for her, she's still very happy she's her own boss.

"The nice thing about running your own business is that when you get bored of something, you can just turn around and try something else that looks fun!" she says.

She admits that over the years some people told her she was too young to build a company (she also ran a dress-making business in high school), but she never let her age hold her back. And she says you shouldn't either.

"If you conduct yourself properly and act professionally, it doesn't matter how old you are. You can do this, too!" says Teang.

TEANG TANG'S
TOP 3 BUSINESS TIPS

1. Come up with a plan

No, that doesn't mean simply dreaming up cool ideas for making candy-coated grasshoppers. (Because, really, are there ever enough flavors to keep everybody happy?) A real business starts with a real business plan. That means writing out your ideas on paper and including things like:

- What will your company offer your customers? Colorful erasers? A new computer app? Snow shoveling?

- Who will your customers be? Aunt Millie and Uncle Jim? Kids in your class? Everybody with red hair?

- How many other companies are a lot like yours? The more competition you have, the harder it will be to make a buck.

- How will you make yours different? Will you offer 31 flavors of grasshopping goodness?

- Who else will run the business? Maybe your best friend wants to get involved. Some kids even start businesses with their siblings. No joke.

- How will you make the company's product or offer the service?

- How are you going to get the word out that your company exists? In other words, how will you advertise?

- What money will you need to get your, say, candied-grasshopper business off the, er, ground?

- How will your company make money? Sounds obvious, doesn't it? But a lot of people start businesses without a clear sense of what they will charge customers and how they will collect their cash.

2. Just do it

For a lot of people, planning is tons of fun, but that's all they do, says Teang. If after you write the business plan, you still think it's a good idea, find a mentor (someone who already runs a business and can offer advice) and take the leap! "It's scary, but be radical. Try something no one else has tried before."

3. Don't be afraid of failure

That's right. Explore. Experiment. Mess up...then learn from your mistakes. That's how a lot of businesspeople eventually find their winning formula (although not everyone will admit it). "Because nothing is failure. If you tried something new, hopefully you'll have learned a lesson and will just try something different the next time around," says Teang.

Free puppy

Who would have guessed that there's such a thing as a "puppy scam" (classified ads that target dog lovers)? Or a "bomb threat scam" (the victim receives an e-mail saying that a bomb has been planted and if she doesn't want it to go off in the building, she has to wire money immediately)? In 2010, the Canadian Anti-Fraud Centre reported that in one month alone, Canadians lost $3.5 million to fraudsters.

FREE RIDE #5: **ALLOWANCE!**

Money for nothing

Just kidding...your allowance is okay. Spend it, save it, do what you want with it. Knock yourself out.

Now back to business

Still wish you could win the lottery? Well, in a way you already have—the birthday lottery! By coming into this world after 1995, about the time when the Internet ka-boomed across the nation, you were born at a really excellent time in history—especially if you want to be your own boss, make your own money, and start your own company. And here's

Kira finds a fake fiver

True story. Not long after I researched counterfeit money for this book, I walked into my local pet store to buy food for my family's hungry guinea pigs. But as soon as I slapped down three $5 bills to pay for it, the eagle-eyed cashier spotted trouble.

"Uh-oh. There's another one," she said.

It turned out that one of my bills was fake—and I'd had no idea! To be fair, the store manager told me it was one of the most realistic forgeries she'd seen in a while. If felt just like real money, and other than the fact that it was missing a metallic stripe and ghost image embedded in the paper (two of the many security features Canadian bills use), the counterfeit fiver was convincing. Still, I was embarrassed I'd missed the telltale signs.

Wondering what you should look out for, too? Visit your country's national bank website to get the lowdown on bogus bills.

why: It's a lot (and I mean a *lot*) cheaper to start many different types of businesses today than it was 20 years ago. We have technology to thank.

Imagine you wanted to start your own yearbook business. You talked to your friends, found out none of the middle schools in your town published yearbooks, and decided people would pay for them (for no other reason than to feed the need to see that great shot of Erica blowing spaghetti out of her nose at lunch).

In the old days

Creating a yearbook took a lot of time, work, and money. You needed cameras to shoot the images and money to develop the photos. If you wanted to advertise your business, you'd have to spend cash on posters or buy newspaper ads. You'd have to find space for all the volunteers or staff you'd need to keep the project hopping. You also had to literally cut and paste the photos and place them on pages to be sent to a printer, which, by the way, charged a mint. In other words, if you wanted to start your own yearbook company, you needed a lot of capital (fancy-speak for start-up money) to launch it and keep it going.

Now

It's easy enough to grab free, or nearly free, design and layout software online. Digital cameras are generally inexpensive, and there's no developing cost. Your whole office can consist of a desk, a chair, and a computer. As long as a grown-up is kept in the loop, you can use social media sites to spread the word and advertise the service for free. Meanwhile, your website can impress clients. And printing? It's all about print-on-demand, baby. Customers order and pay for the number of books they want, and once you have the money, you print only the ones you've sold. Maybe you decide to avoid printing altogether and post the whole kit-and-caboodle online instead to create a virtual book.

The point is that starting a business today is a lot more doable than ever before. So if you've got a fab idea and like running the show but are worried about jumping in, just remember...the most important thing is to give it a try.

Now, want to find out what you can do with all the hard-earned cash you've made? Here's a clue: It starts with S and ends with P-E-N-D. You'll learn more starting on the next page.

"*I can make more generals, but horses cost money.*"

– ABRAHAM LINCOLN

CHAPTER FIVE

HEY, SMART SPENDER

Get more bang for your bucks!

YOU KNOW THE FEELING. You're walking through the mall or window-shopping downtown, minding your own business, and BAM! Out of the clear blue sky some wonderful whatchamacallit beckons. In no time flat, your nose is against the glass, your body feels all tingly— and you're dreaming about how much better your life would be if you just had *that thing*.

It looks like you've just come down with a bad case of the "want it, need it, gotta have it" syndrome.

Hey, we all know what that feeling is like. Because let's get one thing out in the open right now: Buying stuff is fun. Not only are stores set up to make shopping enjoyable (hello, flattering lighting and awesome music), but you get to go home with a new pair of snappy shoes or the latest video game and blast your way to extra levels.

What's more, spending also keeps the economy pretty healthy. For example, even when you buy something as simple as a bag of popcorn...

- The corn farmer makes money.

- So do the people who print the bag it comes in.

- And don't forget the guy who sold it to you. He keeps his job.

- If he works, he's got money to spend on a new pair of skates.

- If he buys a pair of skates, the people who stitched them together make a salary, too.

And so it goes, on and on. In short, without spending, businesses of all kinds are in trouble and people lose jobs.

(Don't) go for broke

But there's also a dark side to spending money—especially if you spend too much. Or spend unwisely. In most cases, the key to this is learning how to ignore (or at least bargain with) that "want it, need it, gotta have it" syndrome we all suffer from. Easier said than done? Let's start by taking a look at one of our biggest spending issues. I call it lotsa-stuff-itis.

But economists call it over-consumption.

Don't open the door!

The door of your closet, that is. Because if you're like most people in the Western world today, your cabinets and drawers are probably chockablock full of stuff you no longer wear or need. Seventeen sweaters? Check. Eleven pairs of shoes? Check. A stack of old toys and gadgets as high as your nose? Okay, you'll cop to that, too. It's not just that you've outgrown these items (although you may have). It's that you've simply become bored with them, or frankly, never really needed them in the first place. It's called over-consumption, and it's on the rise.

In 1900, we, the people of Earth, spent **$1.5 trillion** on stuff.* Sounds like a big number, right?

But in 1975 that number grew to **$12 trillion**.

And in 1998, it doubled to **$24 trillion**.

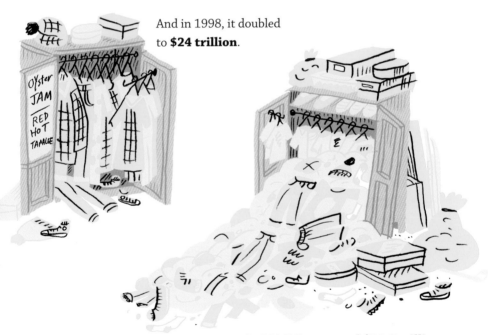

In 2006? It was a cool **$30.5 trillion**. And it keeps going up!

---

* So what exactly is "stuff"? In this case, it generally means everything that we buy—even the essential items, such as food or clothes. Just as people can buy lots of books or toys they don't need, a family can also buy more groceries than they need to survive.

What's the difference between consumerism and consumption?

Shop til ya Drop!

Good question. **Consumption** is all about buying things that we need in order to survive. Warm clothes in cold climates. Food for the week. **Consumerism**, however, focuses on things we want. Five winter coats, for instance, or a specific brand of cereal that we saw on a TV commercial that looked cool. When you hear people talk about North America's "consumer culture," they're talking about our society's love of buying things we want but don't need to live.

But what does it all mean?

Pretty big numbers, right? But couldn't the spike in consumption just be chalked up to there being more people and money on the planet? That seems logical, doesn't it?

Let's run some numbers. In 1900, there were 1.6 billion people on the planet. In 2006, there were four times that amount: 6.5 billion. So sure, there are more people on the planet with money to spend today, but not over *20 times* as many (as in $1.5 trillion x 20 = $30 trillion).

Plus, the places on the planet that have experienced the biggest increases in population during this time are poorer countries where people can't afford to buy much stuff anyway. In other words, they're not responsible for this over-consumption boom.

According to the United Nations and World Watch, the U.S. and Canada, with just over 5 percent of the world's population, are responsible for 31.5 percent of consumption. South Asia, with 22.4 percent of the population, is responsible for 2 percent of consumption. Meanwhile, the poorest 20 percent of the world's people account for just 1.3 percent of the total global spending by citizens.

What about inflation, you ask? Don't many items cost more (a lot more) now than they did 100 years ago? True. There's no question that these rising prices have also had an effect on consumerism rates. But not even the effect of inflation is enough to account for the total spike in growth. Straight up, North Americans buy a lot of stuff.

What's wrong with loving our stuff?

Nothing as long as you don't mind the fact that at the current rate of consumption, we're digging the equivalent of 112 Empire State Buildings' worth of material every day to make it all. That's one big bite we're collectively chomping out of the earth.

The truth is, overbuying isn't bad only for our wallet—it's tough on the environment, too.

It's easy. Just add money!

So how did we end up here? Why *do* we buy so much? Here are a few of the reasons.

One home, two piles of money

Does your mom hit the road with a cup of coffee in hand while you head off to school? In January 2010, it finally happened: There were more women than men in the workforce in the U.S. (In Canada it happened even earlier, in 2009.) That's a big jump from 1950, when only one out of every three women worked.

Because more families have two parents bringing home the bacon, they have more disposable income. (And no, "disposable income" doesn't mean money you can throw away. It's the money leftover after you pay taxes, silly.) More income means more money. And more money means the ability to buy more stuff, at least as long as the two earners make enough to keep up with inflation.

Now, hold on—no one is saying we should blame girls for wanting to make money. (Hey, if I felt that way this book never would have been written...at least not by me.) Besides, studies have shown that people who work are happier with their lives than those who don't. Still, the whole two-income reality has an impact on how much we buy.

The result: More money coming into the family means more money can be spent.

Globalization gone wild

The apples in your juice were grown in China. Your shirt was made in Thailand. And Indian factory workers stitched up your pencil case. You'd think with all this whizzing around the planet, these products would cost more in the store, not less. But many companies at home now use

We bought this?

Here are just a few bizarre, real-life products out there for you to consider: Think Thanksgiving turkeys should have more than one wishbone? That little oversight vexed Ken Ahroni, too. Now he's the president of Lucky Break Wishbone Corp. in Seattle, Washington, a company that makes plastic wishbones that snap!

Here's an idea: Let's make goggles for dogs and sell them online! Oh, wait. That's already been done. Now Doggles are popping up on canine peepers near you.

Speaking of dogs, some people actually pay to slip into a silky coat of dog hair. Fans say dog hair spun into yarn, (a.k.a. chiengora) is warm and repels water. Could that be because it makes you want to shake vigorously after walking in the rain?

$125 for a bar of soap? What's in it, silver? Actually yes, that's exactly what Cor silver soap contains. The people who make it say it kills bacteria and makes skin look younger. (Psst! So does regular washing and using sunscreen daily.)

companies in countries that pay workers much less than your mom or dad would make here.

The result: Cheaper stuff to buy. So we buy more of it.

Chaaaarge it!

Ah, the credit card. It's tempting to slap a little plastic card down to pay for groceries, haircuts, and nail polish. They can be really convenient. But that's the problem. Credit cards can make shopping a little *too* easy. Studies have actually shown that we buy more stuff if we use a credit card instead of cash.

The result: It seems plastic takes the sting out of spending when you're paying with it because, well, it doesn't look like real money.

So now we know why we can afford to buy so much—and that our spending is a tad out of control. Which leads to the next burning question: why do we buy *what* we buy? Before we find the truth behind that one, I'd like you to meet someone first.

Doing what comes irrationally

He's logical by day and rational by night! He only thinks about himself, no matter what! And he doesn't let his feelings, emotions, or physical pains get in the way of meeting his financial goals of tomorrow! Who is this masked monetary superhero?

He's **Rational Man**—the guy traditional economists turn to when they want to determine how people make decisions. Sounds great, doesn't he?

There's only one problem: He doesn't actually exist.

Who says Rational Man doesn't exist?

Well, every behavioral economist* on the planet, actually. While more traditional economists assume that people are rational and will always do what's best for them—like get enough sleep when they're tired, buy low and sell high, or even pick the best-tasting can of soda—behavioral economists assume only one thing...

People are complex creatures who often do stupid things that make no sense at all. So who's right? Let's take a look at some evidence.

PEOPLE ACT STRANGE, EXAMPLE #1
HERE, TASTE THIS...

A bunch of researchers headed to a California grocery store and set up a tasting booth. On one day they put out six different kinds of jam. When they returned on other days, they loaded up the table with 24 varieties.

On the 24-jam jar days the table was

Unlike neoclassical or classical economists—people who study how the economy works and try to predict the future—newfangled behavioral economists are more of a mishmash between economist and psychologist. They look at human behavior as they try to understand how people handle money.

hopping. So many colors! So much choice! But despite what classic economic theory tells us—that more choice is better for the consumer—only 3 percent of people actually bought a jar that day. And on the six-jar day? A whopping 30 percent of tasters swiped a jar and took it to the checkout counter.

Too much choice isn't a good thing. It's just confusing.

PEOPLE ACT STRANGE, EXAMPLE #2
HOME, SMALL HOME

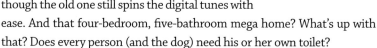

It's not just jam that has us reaching for our wallets when we normally wouldn't. We spring for all sorts of things we don't really need. Maybe it's another sweater when we already have 12. Or it's a new iPod, even though the old one still spins the digital tunes with ease. And that four-bedroom, five-bathroom mega home? What's up with that? Does every person (and the dog) need his or her own toilet?

It turns out, most of us don't even *want* that much space. Not on a gut level, anyway. That's what Colin Ellard, an experimental psychologist from the University of Waterloo, found out after he ran an experiment in his research lab. He had home buyers and real estate agents slap on virtual reality headsets and then walk around the school gymnasium.

The headsets were programmed to make people feel like they were strolling through three different houses: one designed by famous architect Frank Lloyd Wright; a cozy, smaller home; and finally a huge new monster home. After these fake tours, the people were asked a bunch of questions that would reveal which home they liked best.

Although many people assumed the big, rich-looking house would take first place, it didn't. Instead, the comfy house, although small, was the hands-down winner.

"It's not the size of the house that makes you feel comfortable. It's the layout and design," says Colin.

So why are so many new homes built to be bigger than typical families need? Remember, we often think more is better. And don't forget that little thing called peer pressure. If everybody else seems to be snatching up jumbo mansions, shouldn't you, too? Turns out the answer is yes—even if it means paying too much money for rooms and space you don't really need (or even want!).

Ad-ing it Up

So our buying habits can be a little kooky. Even a little emotional. How else to explain why your dad comes home with a tub of peanut crunch ice cream when he's had a bad day at work?

But there's more. Traditional economics may have been slow to figure out why we spend money, but advertisers have been inside our heads for a long time.

PEOPLE ACT STRANGE, EXAMPLE #3
TAKE THE TASTE-TEST CHALLENGE!

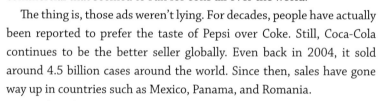

So here's some homework for you. Check out YouTube and search for old television ads where people are in a blind taste test for Coke and Pepsi. Here's the gist of them: Without knowing which one was which, the intrepid tasters tried them both and declared Pepsi the winner. It was a big-time commercial that seemed to run for eons all over the world.

The thing is, those ads weren't lying. For decades, people have actually been reported to prefer the taste of Pepsi over Coke. Still, Coca-Cola continues to be the better seller globally. Even back in 2004, it sold around 4.5 billion cases around the world. Since then, sales have gone way up in countries such as Mexico, Panama, and Romania.

But that doesn't makes sense, you say? No, it doesn't. Remember Rational Man on page 58? If people were actually more like him, we would find out which soda pop we like the taste of best, then buy only that kind.

So what's going on? It's time to enter the world of **neuromarketing**, a new science-advertising cross that uses cutting-edge brain research to figure out what makes us buy. This is some "brand" new science.

Sounds creepy

Relax, no brains were harmed in the making of any commercial. Instead, an American researcher wired up about 70 volunteers to a special machine during a cola taste test. Using the machine, he was able to see what areas of the brain would react as people slurped the sodas. Again, Pepsi was the hands-down winner with more brains displaying the "this *feels* awesome" reaction on his computer screen.

But here's the thing: When he tried the experiment again with the labels showing, suddenly a bunch of pro-Pepsi drinkers switched sides to Coke. That time the *thinking* section of the brain lit up.

What the classic study seemed to prove—and other neuromarketing studies have since—is that brand is an extremely powerful force. In fact, it's so powerful, it has the ability to make us choose a product we don't even really like the taste, feel, or look of.

But here's what we *do* like: how we picture ourselves using it.

What does "brand" mean?

Close your eyes and say these words to your self: Apple. Gucci. Reebok. Notice how the words suddenly became images in your mind? Advertisers spend a lot of time and money giving some gizmo, purse, or running shoe a whole story that they want us to relate to.

Because if that product's story speaks to us on a gut level, we're more likely to pony up the cash to buy it.

It's all about who you know

Given this fact, it's no wonder advertisers are slapping their brand logos on everything from pencils to banner ads. Because here's something else they know: people buy the brands they recognize.

For example, take another taste-test study from researchers at Stanford University in the United States. They gave a bunch of kids the same french fries and chicken nuggets wrapped up in different packages.

COUNT MONEY = FEEL LIKE A MILLION BUCKS

Believe it or not, spending is not the only way that money can bring us a happy rush. Researchers from Chinese and American universities discovered that merely *thinking* about money and handling it is enough to make us feel better.

In one experiment, the team asked some people to count eighty $100 bills. Other people counted eighty worthless pieces of paper. After both groups played a video game designed to make them feel crummy about themselves, the participants who counted the real McCoy were still feeling relatively groovy.

Not only that, they even reported feeling less pain when their fingers were plunged in hot water for 30 seconds. Eek!

The ones offered in McDonald's wrappers got the biggest thumbs-up. Remember, same food, just a recognizable brand—a brand millions of people love and trust. Those feelings go a long way.

You're a tween? We love you!

Sorry to be the one to tell you, but advertisers have got you pegged, and they're totally after your money. Kids between the ages of eight and 14 (all, say, 20 million of y'all in the U.S.) have got serious spending power. Not only do American tweens—I hate that word, too, but bear with me—walk around with an average of $9 spending money a week, but their parents are out buying stuff for them, too.

Exactly how much money is being spent is tough to pin down, since there are quite a few numbers floating around. But one company, 360Youth.com, reports that

- tweens spend $51 billion (others rank it as $43 billion)
- parents shell out $170 billion more for them

Girls are especially prized by advertisers and marketers, since they're the ones spending the most money or convincing Mom to open her wallet. In fact, some experts say that girls are the most powerful consumer group since the baby boom. To reflect this demographic switch, there's been a shift in the ad industry over the past decade, too. A bunch of new companies are springing up saying they've got the power to turn girl-speak into biz-speak.

And just check out these book titles: *The Great Tween Buying Machine: Capturing Your Share of the Multi-Billion-Dollar Tween Market,* or *What Kids Buy: The Psychology of Marketing to Kids.* Any way you look at it, advertisers know an opportunity when they see one.

All this attention has been enough to warrant launching stores and services aimed specifically at you. Build-a-Bear, Paint Your Own Pottery, and American Girl are just a few examples of these original retailers. Meanwhile, companies with massive kid appeal, like Disney and Nickelodeon, have been known to offer cellphone ringtones for the wave of "starter phones" on the market for kids and teens.

But is there anything actually wrong with making stuff specifically for kids to buy? On one hand, no, of course not. Who wants to wear clothes that look like something a mom would wear?

The problem is, advertising isn't about *making* stuff for kids, it's about *selling* stuff to kids. And sometimes what advertisers are selling is just a bunch of hot air.

Label it any way you want

Take labels on clothing, for example. Those labels have a lot of power because advertisers spend time, energy, and money to make sure they tell a story. Remember what you just read a few pages back about brand? Same idea. Apparently, some stories are worth more than others.

Are you possessed by constant cravings?

Last week you wanted a new bike. This week you can't stop thinking about that commercial you saw on TV. Welcome to the cycle of wanting and spending—economists call it "the hedonistic treadmill." This is what it looks like:

- You decide you really want that new T-shirt, poster, digital thingy...
- Finally you buy it (or convince Dad to flash his cash after using a hefty dose of pester power).
- You feel excited and happy! But...
- ...within a day, a week, or a month, that thrill goes away.
- You feel empty and want to buy something new so you can feel excited and happy all over again.
- Now you decide that what you really want is a new sweater, or a trip to Disneyworld, or an awesome watch that transforms into a robot.
- The cycle continues...

She's been a model, architect, businesswoman, and mom. But it was a little newspaper article that turned Gracie Cavnar's life topsy-turvy and made it go in a whole new direction. The 1996 article mentioned that Texas schools were putting in pop machines, and Gracie, who had also spent years in the marketing business, knew she had to stop them.

"I knew exactly what the junk-food manufacturers were doing," she says today. "A five-year-old is a very inexpensive get. If you start drinking Pepsi at five, you'll be drinking Pepsi at fifty. It will cost a fortune to get Coke to convince you to switch when you're older, but it costs nothing to hook a five-year-old."

Today she's not only convincing schools to give up sugary drinks in the halls, but also running the Recipe for Success Foundation, which teaches students how to grow, cook, and then eat their own food. She's even launching Hope Farms, a 100-acre organic farm in downtown Houston—the largest city farm in the world!

"We do what we can to empower kids' taste buds," she says. No cola, or advertising, required.

Let's compare two pairs of jeans, okay?

What do you think? The more expensive jeans are way cooler, right? They're probably even more well made. But what if I told you they were put together in the exact same factory, using the exact same materials, by the exact same people? The only difference: that label stitched onto the back. (Which apparently is worth $55. Yup, 55 smackeroos.)

True story. I used to work at a moderately expensive clothing store that sold clothes and underwear to girls and women. We had nice lighting, pretty decor, and a lot of staff to help customers out. And it turned out we sold a few pieces of clothing that were *exactly the same* as clothes in other stores in the mall. Side by side, you'd never know the difference. You would have had to look in the neck hole to find the label in order to suss out which store made which garment.

The first time I stumbled across a shirt like that, I couldn't believe it. The el-cheapo store down the hall was hawking it for about $30 less than we were! Was there a catch?

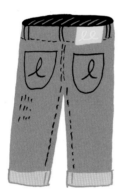 

JEANS #1:
Bought at:
Cut-rate Clothing
Cost: $32

JEANS #2:
Bought at:
Super-awesome Clothiers
Cost: $87

It turns out that when buyers (the people who help decide what stores will sell each season) go to purchase merchandise, they'll often go to the same sellers or factories as other buyers. And they'll sometimes pick the same shirts, pants, or other products. Then, in many cases, stores will pay the factory to attach their own labels before shipping them to their warehouses.

The cost of cool

So how does a company decide whether to charge $32 or $87? **Here's the short answer:** they'll try to charge whatever we're willing to pay. Sometimes that tactic works for them. The items fly off the shelves no matter what. (Remember the Apple iPad?) Sometimes it doesn't and the store has to mark the items down on sale.

Still, there are a lot of different factors that go into price-point decision making.

Covering the costs
Maybe the company pays staff a little better than others in the industry and offers lots of training, or maybe they shell out a lot of dough to make the stores look nice. They'll probably need to jack up the prices on their products to pay for that. At the same time, these companies know that if they improve lighting and make sure their stores look neat and inviting, customers will assume the product is better, too, and they'll pony up the cash to pay for it.

More expensive = better?
Then there's the price itself. It turns out that many consumers assume a high price means the product is better than the lower-priced one. It's a weird but effective circular argument: "Charge more and they'll pay more, so you can charge more." (I know, it hurts my brain, too.)

Grown-ups are so clueless
Your parents might come across this issue at the dinner table tonight if they crack open a bottle of wine. That's because numerous studies have shown that people don't necessarily enjoy expensive wine any more than they do a cheap bottle—they only think they do *because it's more expensive*. In fact, one study that looked at 6,000 blind tasting results found that people, on average, enjoy pricy wine slightly less!

Another study conducted by the California Institute of Technology and Stanford's business school looked at adults' brain scans when drinking two glasses of wine. The researchers were examining the brain's pleasure center when the subjects took a taste from each cup, thinking one was filled with $90 wine and the other filled with $10 wine. But here's what the subjects didn't know: The wines actually came from the same cheap bottle. When the people sipped from the "expensive" cup, more blood and oxygen rushed to the medial orbitofrontal cortex—a decision-making part of the brain. People were analyzing it more thoroughly, looking for the improved flavors. But nothing at all was different between that glass of wine and the other. Just the imagined price.

Money well spent?

So what does this all mean in the end? Is shopping a lot of fun? Absolutely. I'm a fan, too.

But it pays to think about **what you're spending money on and why** the next time you're itching to part with some cash at the checkout counter. You might decide there are there are better things to spend your money on.

Okay, now that you're the "I" in "I spend smart," it's time to charge over to Chapter 6. (Yup, that's a clue.)

"*I'd say it's been my biggest problem all my life...it's money. It takes a lot of money to make these dreams come true.* "

– WALT DISNEY

CHAPTER SIX

THIS PLASTIC LIFE

Or why spending imaginary money can be just as tricky as it sounds

JUST BECAUSE A SHOP wants to sell you a $300 pair of shoes, it doesn't mean you have the money to buy it. Bummer, right? But what would happen if a friend offered to *lend* you money to cover the cost if you promised to pay it back? Would you say yes?

Okay. Now what if it wasn't a friend offering you the money but a credit card company? And as you paid the money back, you also had to pay something called "interest"?

Still sound like a good deal? Before you say yes this time, here are a few things you need to know about credit.

Debt

Money you owe somebody or some institution (such as a bank), usually because you've borrowed it from them in the past.

"Can I have a credit card, Mom? Please?"

Not so fast. Although it seems everybody's whipping out plastic every time you turn around—at the mall, in restaurants, online, and even in the air—credit has a way of turning into a big balance. At the time of writing this book, American citizens had $2.45 trillion in consumer debt!

May I interest you in interest rates?

One of the main reasons credit-card debt spirals out of control comes down to one word: interest. That's a kind of fee credit-card companies—*issuers* is actually the right word—charge you for borrowing money from them. If they make you pay 15 percent interest and you spend $100 on some fancy goldfish, scooter, or new necklace, you're out an extra $15 if you don't pay up by the end of the year.

Give them a break

Absolutely, credit-card companies should charge us some kind of fee if we don't pay back the money when we say we will. After all, by loaning out the cash, they're taking a risk. It's only fair.

Question: What was the first popular credit card made out of?

John Doe
0000 0000 0000

a) Paper

b) Plastic

c) Cardboard

d) Cloth

Answer: c) Cardboard. In 1950, Diners Club offered its first card to be used at 27 restaurants in New York City. Within one year, nearly 20,000 Americans had them in their wallets. Move ahead to the end of 2009. There were 576.4 million (plastic) credit cards in America, and people had used them over 20 billion times!

Compound you, credit cards!

But the problem with credit-card fees is that the issuers don't simply charge interest at the end of each year. They charge it each month, and the interest compounds.

(Deep breath now. This whole compounding thing is easier to understand than it seems.)

For example, let's take that $100. A month's worth of interest is $1.25 ($1.25 x 12 months = $15). Because the interest compounds, the next month you're paying interest on $101.25. After a while the extra cents really add up.

But Dad always pays the minimum balance!

The credit-card issuers must love him. He's their perfect client. He pays some of his loan (or principal) on time, but pays plenty of interest, too. How much? If he borrows $5,000 and makes the 2 percent minimum payments per month, it will take him **32 years** to pay it off! Not only that, he'll also pay $7,789.56 in interest.

Suddenly, that $5,000 has cost your family $12,789.56. In debt terms, dear old Dad is a "revolver," someone whose debt cycle just keeps going around and around in circles—and keeps making the credit-card company money! To avoid this nutty schedule, he should pay off bigger chunks each month. But even if he does increase the size of his payments, your dad is now living with something called debt. D-E-B-T: It's amazing how those four little letters can cause such a ruckus for you, me...even entire countries.

Buy now, pay later

Debt can be a good thing. Nearly everyone at one point in their life goes into some kind of debt when they borrow money to get something quite expensive that they can't pay for all at once—such as a home or a car. And over time, most people pay these loans back. But debt can also be a big drag if we're not careful. When that happens, a family can be sucked down into a vortex of debt and have a really hard time getting out of it. Some people even have to declare bankruptcy.

But this definitely doesn't have to happen to you. Imagine you decide to go to university or college but don't have all the money you need to pay for tuition, books, housing, and food. You can apply for a student loan. (Just ask your school counselor where to go to get the papers to apply or how to apply online. Or hit your favorite bank. It's an easy and common process.) This is known as a good debt because it's going to help you get a better job and earn a better salary someday. In the long run, you'll be better off with the education than without it.

Just one word of warning: Pay your student loan back on time, or you could end up paying a lot more than you bargained for. If you don't get a job after school right away, go to the bank. In some cases, they can give you a little more breathing room before you have to pay.

WHAT'S A CREDIT RATING?

How can an institution that gives you a loan know you're not going to take the money and run? It's impossible to tell for sure, but they can examine your credit rating, or score, and determine the likelihood you'll pay the money back.

A credit rating is made up of complicated statistical information gathered from all the loans you've taken out before. If you paid them back on time, your credit score number goes up. If you didn't pay back a loan or were late with payments, your number goes down.

Scores are measured between 600 and 900. Any number below 650 is considered "poor" and you'll have a hard time getting another loan. If you hit 750 and up, you've got a "great" rating.

Everybody, get down!

Sometimes when people get a big loan, they don't borrow *all* the money they need to buy an item. Instead, they present a large chunk of money toward the price called a down payment. For example, if you're buying a $17,000 car, you might offer a $5,000 down payment and borrow the remaining $12,000 with a loan. Obviously, the bigger the down payment, the better.

So good you're bad

Clearly, mishandling credit cards and loans can be a little scary. So let's say you decide you're smarter than that. There'll be nothing but full, on-time payments for you! You'll be the perfect customer, right? Actually...in the topsy-turvy credit world, good customers like you can actually be considered bad.

Huh?

Think of it this way. Unlike the beloved "revolvers"—people who owe lots of money, pay lots of interest, but don't default (stop paying entirely)—people who pay off their entire balance every month are considered a disaster! They're borrowing money but not paying any interest. No interest equals no money for the credit-card people. And because other credit-card companies can check in and see this awesome track record—also known as a credit rating—the next time these responsible people try to get another card they might be told, "No way!"

I'm willing to pay anything

Researchers discovered that people were willing to pay twice as much for basketball tickets when they used a credit card instead of paying cash. Credit-card spending just doesn't feel like real money. There are a lot of other emotional reasons that make us overspend, too.

- We want to look as cool as everybody else.
- We're bored.
- It's fun to get new stuff.
- Money is power. When we spend it, we feel strong!
- We have a lot of money, so we spend it. What's the big deal?
- We don't have a lot of money, so when we get some we want to spend it right away.

Whether we're trying to fit in, feel good, or just give ourselves a little extravagant treat, credit cards allow us to take chances we would never normally consider if we could only pay for things with cash.

Credit + good times = a bubble bath?

Even though credit cards can turn a little debt into a big problem, very few of us actually have a poor credit rating. Most fall into the "great" range. The truth is that even though it's easy to rack up tons of debt, most people know their limits and don't spend more than they earn.

But sometimes, even the most level-headed folks end up getting into debt, especially if everybody seems to be splurging. Throughout history, it's been during the very, VERY good times (called bubbles) that people have gone the most money crazy—and usually been left with empty wallets. In other words, they take a bath. Here's what I mean:

Terrible tulip tragedy

Gives new meaning to "flower power."
From 1620 to 1637 people in Holland went wacky for tulips. Professional tulip traders were soon selling them for thousands of gold florins (coins). People swept up by the craze traded their homes, horses, and carriages for the bulbs. Farmers, maids, and chimney sweeps even quit their jobs to buy bulbs in hopes that they could sell them at a higher price later. But in 1637 the bubble burst, and in the end those prized tulips made people dirt poor.

South Sea Company goes south

Here, let me help pay—but it's going to cost you...
Britain was in debt after jumping into the War of the Spanish Succession. Luckily the South Sea Company agreed to finance the debt on two  conditions: The Brits had to pay interest, and South Sea would be the only company allowed to trade with the Spanish Americas. For ordinary folks, investing money in the powerful company sounded like a sure bet. Only one problem: By 1720, South Sea had lost its ships...as well as all of the cash that people invested in the company!

Yukon almost taste the riches!

"From a land where the streets seem lined with gold..."
On August 16, 1896, three eagle-eyed men found lumps of gold in a Yukon creek in northern Canada. Word got out the next spring, and within one short year, tens of thousands of men, women, and kids had

arrived to strike gold, too. Sourdoughs, as the prospectors were called, swatted at swarms of bugs in the summer and braved horrific cold and avalanches in the winter. And for what? While a few of the first people got rich, by 1898 nearly all the gold seekers had left—without gold.

Depression is so depressing

What a shock to the system.
After the horror of the First World War, the twenties were downright exciting. With new technology everywhere— such as radios and improved cars—and a general feeling of happiness, what better time to invest money in the stock market? But the optimism couldn't last forever. When share prices started falling, some people panicked and cashed in their investments. Then more people. And more. On October 29, 1929, shares dropped like a stone, making people's investments worthless. Hello, Great Depression.

It just didn't compute

If I tack an "e" on the name, everyone will buy it!
In the mid- to late-1990s, the world was going gaga over tech companies. The web as we know it today was brand-spanking new and loads of people wanted to invest their money in companies that they hoped would be the next Google or eBay. The problem was that people, not knowing which one would be the Next Big Thing, were throwing their money at any e-company with a half-baked idea. By 2000 reality sunk in, and most of the tech companies scaled way back or tanked—the e-boom went bust. Again, people who invested in these failed companies lost it all.

Mansions gone wrong

I'm richer than I think!
Housing bubbles pop up again and again, but the bubble of 2008 was downright wild. For a few years, financial folks played fast and loose with loans—lending anyone with a pulse lots of money to buy a house—as long as they were willing to pay it off with interest over 30, 40, or even 50 years (far longer than the usual 15- to 20-year periods of times past). With so many new people waving cash around, housing prices went sky high...and still people kept buying homes. Eventually, too many people couldn't pay their mortgages (loans), and the whole housing industry went kaput.

What did all those situations have in common?

One word: over-optimism.

Let's say we have a glass that's filled up halfway with juice. If you're an optimistic person, you'll probably say it's half full. The more pessimistic bunch will say the glass is half empty. But what happens if someone is *overly optimistic*? He'll tell you the glass isn't just half full—he's convinced that at any moment someone's going to come along and fill it up to the top!

For some crazy reason people have a really hard time learning from old mistakes. We think: "The Great Depression? Hey, that was back in 1929! Our situation in Future Land is completely different." But guess what? We might be wearing different clothes, listening to different music, and eating different snacks at school, but when it comes to racking up debt, we're sadly just as good at it as we were back then. Maybe even better.

No matter what year we live in, these economic bubbles start because overly optimistic people assume great things are on the horizon. They think what they buy today will be worth more tomorrow.

Boom and bust—in 5 easy steps!

1 On Monday a kid in your class shows up with a bag of marbles. By the end of recess he has his buddies convinced they're awesome.

2 The next day those friends show up with their own marbles. Suddenly these little glass balls seem a lot more valuable than they once did.

3 By Thursday the whole class wants in on this marble action. Some even show up with their allowance and offer to pay cash. Now a regular cat's-eye is going for two bucks! Everybody's worried that if they don't buy today, that price will be even higher tomorrow.

4 Eventually the kids run out of money to spend. So marble prices drop. But here's the thing—the first group of marble-lovers made money because they didn't spend much, but anyone who paid the higher price later in the week is out lots of cash.

5 The marble craze bubble is officially busted.

What you buy has an impact

SEARCH FOR GREAT DEALS THAT WILL MEAN A GREAT DEAL TO OTHER PEOPLE AND THE PLANET!

A better burger. Make your own hamburgers at home using meat from your local butcher and they'll cost about the same amount as the ones you eat at big hamburger chains starting with the letters "M" and "C." Farmers near you will thank you.

Righteous rugs. Looking for a new carpet for your room? Choose one with a GoodWeave label. To earn the label, carpet exporters and importers pledge not to employ kids under age 14 and to pay fair wages to adults. Since the program launched in 1995, experts estimate that the number of kids working on South Asia's carpet looms has dropped from 1 million to 250,000.

Bogus bottled water. Thirsty? Bypass bottled water and fill up a reusable bottle instead. Not only will you keep bottles out of the landfill, but you'll save money, too. Drinking the recommended daily amount of water using bottled water will run you about $1,400 a year. Good old tap water? Try 50 cents.

Cheap clothes not cheap. That $9 pair of shoes looks like a great deal...but probably not for the people who made them. In order to make a product that inexpensive, someone probably had to cut corners.

Gas guzzling's got to go. The British spend more for their petrol—that's gasoline to you, cowboy—than people in North America. Why? Taxes. Although grown-ups grumble about paying the taxman, where would we be without him? Taxes pay for your roads, your community pool, your library, and the trees planted outside your home. Taxed gas costs more money, but there's an upside, too. Because Europeans spend more for gas, car companies build cars that use less of it.

It's only fair. Invited to your best friend's birthday and have no idea what to give her? Visit one of the hundreds of fair trade stores around the world (or hop online with a parent to peruse the virtual shelves). These shops buy from small businesses and collectives that treat their employees right. Buy a gift for your friend and you'll give the gift of fairly paid work to someone on the other side of the planet or even close to home.

Smaller house rules. Want your family's dollar to make a big difference? Live in a smaller home. Think less energy and fewer building materials like wood, bricks, and fiberglass. Less space also means fewer pieces of furniture to buy—and toys to pick up!

Wondering how healthy, green, or socially responsible that hand lotion or toaster pastry really is? Trying to decide where to spend your cash? Compare over 65,000 products, the best and worst brands, at www.goodguide.com.

How to purge the urge to splurge

Now we know that spending too much can do a number on our families, our friends, and even our country's economy. So how do we stop plunking down our hard-earned cash or abusing credit to buy stuff we don't actually need?

TIP #1 Think small. Studies show that when people are asked to focus on the cash in their wallet instead of in their bank account, they spend less. That full piggy bank back home? Repeat after me: "It doesn't exist."

TIP #2 Use your imagination. Here's something I do whenever I'm tempted to buy some new gadget or gizmo: I imagine it in my home, unused and collecting dust. Hey, that's probably what's going to happen to it eventually anyway...

Fraud is no fun

Not long ago I got a call from my credit-card company that went something like this:
"Hi Kira. We just wanted to check something out. Have you been making any purchases in Saudi Arabia lately?"
"Uh, no."
"That's what we thought. So we've frozen your card and will be sending you a new one with a new number."
It turned out that someone had found a way to steal my credit-card number and then tried to use it to buy plane tickets in the Middle East and pay a utility bill in Europe. My card really got around! Luckily, credit-card companies hire smart people who spend their whole day trying to thwart the bad guys—fraudsters—who try to get access to our personal information.
So what are the best ways to foil the credit thieves? (Don't have a credit card yet? You should still pay attention—one day these tips could save you a lot of money and grief!) Never, and I mean NEVER, give your credit-card number out to telemarketers who call your house. Shield the card when you go out so no one can take a photo of the number with their phone. Finally, only shop online with a credit card if you trust the site. (In other words, check with your parents beforehand. Sounds uncool? That's nothing compared to how uncool it is to get *massively* ripped off...)

TIP #3   "But everybody's got one!" Even if it *seems* like everyone at school is snatching up whatever the latest fad happens to be this week, don't believe the hype. Chances are there are a lot more kids who haven't jumped on the bandwagon. Do the math. You might be surprised.

Give yourself some credit

So now that you know credit can get you out of trouble and into trouble, maybe it's time to put all that aside for a while and try—wait for it—saving your money instead! I know. Crazy concept. We're all so used to seeing something we want, buying it, and paying for it later. But as you've just read, with credit, some of us pay for our purchases in more ways than one.

So flip to the next chapter and find out how saving can keep you in the black and even help you buy what you really want.

KIRA EXPLAINS:

Economic Bubbles!

HOW THE MONEY WE SPEND CAN DRIVE A WHOLE COUNTRY AROUND THE BEND

"What happens when a country goes into debt and can't get out of it?"

Welcome to Bubbleland, pop. 500,000. Only 10 years ago, Bubbleland was known for fishing, farming...and not much else.

Until ambitious Bubblelanders noticed booming stock markets around the world and said, "We can do that, too!" So local banks borrowed money from other countries' banks...

...which families in Bubbleland then borrowed as loans. Now they have twice as much money to spend! Soon, they're buying houses, cars, and investing in stocks.

Everybody's on board. Kids are even ignoring their traditional fishing and farming training to learn more about making money, money, money.

But then, a recession hits the world! The local banks' debt is now a big problem. Since families can't pay back their loans...

...the local banks can't pay back those other banks that they borrowed from. The president announces that Bubbleland is now bankrupt!

People panic. Stock prices drop 90 percent. Interest rates skyrocket, making it really hard to pay for all those houses and cars bought with loans during the happy times. Bubbleland currency has no value, so the country can't pay for all the things it imports: food, clothing, cars, toys, and books.

Soon Bubblelanders are losing their jobs and hoarding food and money. Unsold houses line the streets. Some people even burn up their expensive cars for the insurance money.

The International Monetary Fund (see p. 126) lends the country money to get back on its feet, which creates yet another big bill to pay. It's back to fishing and farming.

"In the old days a man who saved money was a miser; nowadays he's a wonder."

– UNKNOWN

CHAPTER SEVEN

BANG
FOR YOUR BUCK

Save now and buy later

CONGRATULATIONS! You're a millionaire! Not only can you buy your friends swanky gifts and stock up on your favorite Chippy-Dippy Chipper Pops, but you have cash to pay for toys, sports, music, magazines, and clothes galore. Life is sweet.

Well, all except for the fact that you've suddenly sprouted blue ears, whiskers, and a tail. And that weird guy in a tuxedo running around behind you yelling, "I'm a wrangler! I'm a chicken! No, I'm the king of the world!"

Aw, man, hold on: Is this a dream?

Before you tie the knot, here's a short message from our sponsor...

Did you know the typical wedding costs over $20,000 in the United States and Canada? Between the cake, dress, flowers, and music, the bills can really add up. So you can't blame some couples for finding ways to avoid turning the special day into a pile of debt.

But getting advertisers to sponsor your wedding? That's exactly what some brides-to-be are banking on now.

In 2006, one trailblazing couple saved a reported $80,000 by trading their vows in front of a large crowd at a baseball game. They also found sponsors for their rings, the dress, and even the flowers. In fact, so many companies wanted to hawk their wares at the wedding, the couple ended up donating the extra stuff to a charity!

Don't give up. Save up!

Okay, that *was* a dream. But it doesn't *have* to be. If you know the secret to making money the slow and steady way, there's a chance you can be a millionaire someday, too. And you won't have to grow whiskers and a tail to do it.

And even if you aren't thinking quite that big, learning how to set aside your money can help make your life a lot more fun today. Seriously. Sticking money in your piggy bank or your bank account doesn't have to turn you into Mr. or Ms. Miser—someone who spends all their time counting their coins instead of hanging out with friends, taking drum lessons, or snorkeling in the neighbor's pool.

Instead, with a little patience, saving actually gives you more choice about the kind of fun you want to have!

So why doesn't everybody do it?

Good question. Americans and Canadians (not to mention many other people around the world) are now spending more money than they make. Unlike your grandparents, who were taught by their parents to save before spending, today we're much more likely to turn to loans and credit. Then we're stuck paying it off later...with interest. (Remember? Interest is the fee we pay to borrow someone else's money.) It's an expensive way to go. Saving, however, not only makes you money, it saves you even more money in the long run.

Ready to learn the secret to turning a little stash of cash into a big pile of dough? Want to know why savers get ahead in more ways than you would guess? Believe it or not, the same thing that kills us when we abuse credit helps us when we save. That's right: It's interest, and it's time to make it work for you—not against you.

How, you ask? Patience (it's a good saving skill to learn)! All will be revealed. First, let's take a trip back in time…

Don't eat the marshmallow!

You're four years old and going to preschool on some fancy university campus. For some reason you've been asked to step into the game room. It's not much to look at. A table, a chair, and a bell. That's it. But here's something it *does* have: a sticky, sweet, puffy marshmallow sitting on a plate. And it's all yours…only there's one hitch. The big grown-up who offered it to you gave some instructions you're not too happy about.

"You can eat this marshmallow right away. But I'm going to leave this room for a little while. If you wait until I return to eat that marshmallow, I'll give you another one, too," he says.

What would you do? Eat the marshmallow or wait for the second?

It's all about self-control

That's the question researchers tried to answer back in the late 1960s at Stanford University in California with their now famous "marshmallow study." They asked hundreds of little kids to pick a tasty snack from a tray and then recorded how many of them ate it right away, and how many waited for the better deal.

The results were interesting—and hilarious. Some of the kids popped the treat in their mouths before the researchers even left the room. Others picked it up and sniffed it. Some covered their eyes with their hands so they wouldn't look at it. Other kids sat at their desks...and stared.

- Two out of three kids ate the marshmallow.

- One out of three kids was able to resist and waited until the researcher returned about 15 minutes later.

What did it prove?

At first, not much. On the face of it, the results showed that some people can delay gratification (resist temptation) and others can't. It wasn't until about 15 years later that the study became much more interesting—that's when researchers decided to contact many of the original preschoolers and find out how they were doing. What did they discover?

- The kids who didn't eat the marshmallow—the high delayers— were generally doing well in school, had high marks, were more confident. In short, they were a successful bunch.

- The kids who did eat the marshmallow—the low delayers—seemed to have more behavioral problems at home and at school. Their marks were worse, and they had a harder time keeping friends.

For years, psychologists have thought that intelligence was the one-way ticket to success. Now it seems self-control has a big hand in it, too. After all, even whiz kids have to do their homework and hand in their assignments to get good grades!

So what does this have to do with saving money?

In a word, everything. Remember back at the beginning of the book when you read that **money is never just money**? That's because many of the same rules that apply to money apply to other things in our lives. The self-control that these kids used to not eat the marshmallow is the

YOU'RE THE "SELF" IN SELF-CONTROL!

Researchers of the marshmallow study wanted to see if kids could learn to delay gratification. Many of them could—after they learned simple mind tricks. Here are some ways you can practice your self-control:

Fake it. It turns out one of the best ways to deal with temptation is to trick our brains into ignoring what we want. Try this experiment the next time you go to the mall: When you walk by an item you really want, imagine that it's not actually real. Now how much do you want it?

Have a goal. If you really want a pair of new, but pricey, soccer cleats your mom refuses to pay for, you have something to save for. Stick a photo of them beside your piggy bank and you'll be more likely to save the money.

Consider failure. Actually, consider how it will feel if you fail. If you don't work on your class project for science, what will be the consequences? Will your partner be mad at you for ruining her grade, too? Will your teacher give you a bad grade? Sometimes we're so intent on what's happening right now we forget how our actions will make big trouble later on.

Reward yourself. Been studying for over an hour? Grab a marshmallow or something else that will keep you hopping. No one can put off what they love forever...

same self-control they used to study instead of watching TV, or practice piano instead of texting their friends.

And it's also what allows people to save money instead of spending it.

In other words, if you learn how to save your money, you're also exercising a self-discipline that can boost other areas of your life, too.

So pretty sure you're a marshmallow eater rather than a marshmallow saver? Are you doomed? Heck, no. After all, not all of the marshmallow eaters in the Stanford study turned into aimless couch potatoes. A lot of them learned tricks to deal with their emotions and turn off the television to study—or save money instead of spending it right away.

Harness your brainiac powers to uncover new ways to save

So...how much cash do you have stashed? A hundred bucks? A thousand? Nothing? Hey, if you fall into the last category, you're not the only one. It's official. Whether we're kids, moms and dads, or aunts and uncles, we're no longer a nation of savers. According to a Federal Reserve study in the U.S., 43 percent of Americans spend more than they earn. Meanwhile, the Bank of Canada published numbers saying that for every buck a Canadian makes, they spend $1.30.

It turns out that credit—what a lot of people treat as "free money"— makes us *feel* richer than we actually are, so we spend more. But saving money is still important.

1 If you save up *before* you buy a new video game console or violin, you won't be tempted to tack on extra games or a fancy bow to the purchase. You've only got so much money in your pocket, so you won't go into debt.

2 You'll pay no interest to credit-card companies, so the item is a lot cheaper.

3 You'll feel good knowing you're in control of your money. You don't have to pay someone back on a schedule they set for you.

4 You'll have money for what really matters to you—like university or college someday.

Wanted: Not these jobs!

Need another reason to save up? The only other (legit) way to make extra cash is to earn it the hard way. Sometimes, the *really* hard way.

Blow me down. Before he retired, Richard L'Abbé used to blow himself up for a living. No, he wasn't a stuntman. As the president of a company in Ottawa, he just wanted to prove his product—bomb-disposal suits—worked. Wearing full gear, he'd stand only a few feet from four sticks of exploding dynamite. "It really cleans out your sinuses," he's been known to joke.

I'll take that. What happens if multi-millionaires hit hard times and can't pay for their private jets? Call in the airplane repo men! Traveling with just a propeller lock, GPS system, portable radio, and hundreds of keys, they need to track the planes, fly them away—and sometimes deal with pretty angry former owners.

On the road. Again. You'd think reviewing fancy hotels and restaurants would be a dream gig. But for the evaluators—people who decide which ones get four stars or three diamonds for companies like AAA or Mobil—moving from hotel to hotel and city to city can get awfully tiring. Some evaluators are away from home more than 200 nights a year and rank between 800 and 1,000 properties. "You can't do this job and be a nine-to-five person. You can't," says Michel Mousseau, who was an evaluator for years with CAA/AAA.

Weirdly, it's kind of in our culture to indulge without a thought of overspending or waste. And this affects more than just how we deal with our savings.

Open your first bank account

Let's face it, there are better ways to save your money than by stashing it under your mattress. People open bank accounts to keep their money safer and to have a record of their dealings—not to mention earning a little money as interest. All in all, it's a good idea and still the best way to start a relationship with cash. So what should you look for when you open your first account?

Does the bank offer a children's account? These accounts rarely charge you fees to store your money.

No piggy bank required

HERE ARE SOME GREAT WAYS TO SAVE MONEY THAT ARE BETTER THAN STICKING IT UNDER A MATTRESS.

1 Want the latest fashions? If you wait just a few weeks, they can still be yours.

That's how long it typically takes for stores to put clothes on sale to keep the merchandise moving. Sales are a saver's best friends.

2 Invest it in a new business you're starting and make more money!

In other words, spend money to make money! Sound crazy? Think of it this way: If you want to start babysitting to make some extra cash, use your birthday money to take a babysitting course. Or stock up on cool craft supplies for the tots. Soon you'll be known as the babysitter parents turn to. And if you're in demand, you'll be able to charge more money, too. Your birthday money is a gift that keeps on giving!

3 Join a money group or start one with your friends.

Here's how it works: Grab a bag of cookies or other munchies for your first meeting. Everybody writes down a savings goal (maybe yours is to buy that bike your mom can't afford). You'll want to talk about how you plan to get there, too. Cut lawns? Sell your old clothes to consignment stores? Save your allowance and birthday money? It's up to you. Then meet again every month and track your progress. A little friendly competition to be the first to meet your savings goal will keep you and your buds working hard.

4 Brown-bag your lunch (at least twice a week).

Sure, your cafeteria has got the best grilled cheese ever (just don't touch the Salisbury steak), but if you typically spend $4 on lunch in the caf, bringing your own lunch to school just two times will save you $8 a week. That's an extra $300-plus in your pocket at the end of the year.

5 Offer to do something fun for your best friend on his birthday instead of buying a bunch of stuff.

Do you both like fishing, but he doesn't have a rod? Lend him yours and borrow your dad's. You'll have fun and it's free if you dig around the backyard for worms.

6 Find out if your parents will match your savings dollar for dollar.

(You can tell them they would be encouraging good saving habits, don't you know...) For instance, for every $15 you throw into savings, they'd throw in an additional $15, too. Hey, negotiating with your parents is worth a shot!

Checking or savings account? If you plan to move money in and out of the account regularly, a checking account is probably your best bet. If you plan to save your money there for a longer period of time, a savings account will do the trick.

Don't forget to bring money to deposit, a piece of ID, and a parent or guardian who may have to sign some papers, too.

Waste not, want not

Ever wonder why Great-Aunt Bertha gives you the hairy eyeball whenever you don't finish every last pea, noodle, or speck of burger on your plate? Maybe she knows something you don't: people in food-rich nations throw out an incredible amount of food each day.

A few years back, a British study revealed that 30 percent of all the groceries people buy in the U.K. eventually gets tossed in the trash each year. That's nearly seven million tonnes of food—or a pile the size of about a *million* elephants!

Want to save money? Leave begging for food at the grocery store to the dogs and eat up what you've got at home.

Money for nothing?

By now you've learned a whole bunch of new ways to spend less money and save it for things you really want. But is there really such a thing as free money? In a way, the answer is yes. But they're not just giving it away to anybody.

Ready to invest a little time learning about stocks, bonds, and mutual funds? Turn the page to discover more about this interest-ing topic.

"*The safe way to double your money is to fold it over once and put it in your pocket.*"

– FRANK HUBBARD

CHAPTER EIGHT

MAKE MONEY
GROW

Who needs fertilizer when we've got compound interest?

OKAY, TIME TO BACKTRACK A LITTLE: Remember how in Chapter 2 we were talking about how money doesn't grow on trees? Or in Chapter 4 about how there's no such thing as a free ride in the moneymaking world? Well, those statements weren't lies—technically, both of those things are true. But...

...if there's anything that comes close to either a money tree or a free ride, it's *investing*.

You can think of investing as saving—but with extra oomph! So are you ready to *plant* yourself down, learn how to use compound interest, and do some math? (C'mon, you didn't think you'd pick up a book about money and not have to use your math brain, did you? Relax, this is going to be painless.)

97

It's like magic!

Magic. That's how a lot of people describe compound interest when they're saving or investing their money for the long haul. Because while it's true that compound interest is evil on a credit-card bill, it's incredible when it's working for you and your investments.

And here's why: it can turn $1,000 into a million bucks! Not a word of a lie. In order to make that happen, all you need are three things:

1. Money (a seed in soil)

2. Interest (fertilizer, sun, and rain)

3. Time

When you grow a lettuce plant on your window ledge or in your garden, the process is pretty simple. You take a seed, add stuff that will make it grow, walk away, and—poof!—when you come back there's a seedling. Here's the cool part. You can either pick it right then for a tasty, tiny snack, or leave and come back in a few weeks. By then, that plant is perfect, as long as the growing conditions were still good while you were away. And into the salad bowl it goes.

The same applies to money. Put it into an investment, add an interest rate and some time, and voilà! More money.*

Coin the phrase

Before we go any further, now is a great time to explain a few financial concepts, words, and phrases.

INVESTMENT

Ever hear the old saying "You've got to spend money to make money"? That couldn't be more true than with investing. An investment is something you pay money into with the expectation that someday you'll turn a profit and make even more money.

But just what is this "something" you're investing your money in? Turns out, it can be a few things...

---

*Well, sometimes. Like that lettuce plant, without proper growing conditions, an investment could also shrivel up...and die. But we can come back to this point in a minute.

INVESTMENT #1: **STOCK**

A share of stock is actually a piece of a company. If you own a share of a popular toy company and they release a new game everybody wants, the company will make a profit—and so will you!

INVESTMENT #2: **BOND**

A bond is a debt that companies actually sell. Sounds kooky? Think of it this way. If an ice cream company is having a hard time selling its chilly product in the winter, it could sell bonds to generate money for the slow months. People like you and me buy the bonds for, say, $10 each with the understanding that come busy summertime, the company will pay us back plus give us interest. Both governments and companies offer bonds.

INVESTMENT #3: **MUTUAL FUND**

This is a whole bunch of stocks and bonds together. The theory is if you buy a mutual fund, you won't be sinking all your money into one company. You spread the joy (and the risk) around. If one of the companies tanks, the others will hopefully still be doing okay, so you won't lose as much. Sometimes it works, and sometimes it doesn't.

INVESTMENT #4: **RETIREMENT FUND**

These are funds you use to pay for your retirement (yes, as in "when you don't have to work anymore"). In the U.S., they're called a 401K; in Canada, they're called an RRSP. Whatever you call them, they're a good way to save money for the long, long haul. That's because you often end up paying less tax on the money, plus employers sometimes stick money in the account for you, too.

Run the numbers

Regardless of how you invest your money, let's take a closer look at how an investment works. Say you've been sticking your birthday money and allowance in a jar for a while. You've got $100. Now imagine that you ask your parents to invest it for you. They pick something that gives you an **annual growth rate of 10 percent**. In other words, at the end of the year you'll have $110. Pretty sweet, because you didn't have to do anything at all to make that extra $10. Just sit tight and wait.

But what happens after five years, 10 years, or even 25 or 50 years?

Year 1:	Year 5:	Year 10:	Year 25:	Year 50:
$110	$161.05	$259.37	$1,083.47	$11,739.09

If you're 12 years old now, by the time you're 62, that $100 bill will be worth over $11,700! That's because you don't just make interest on your money, you make interest on your interest, too. So the more money you make, the more it grows. Sure, inflation will mean that money won't be worth as much in 50 years, but it will still be worth much more than the $100 you started with.

Now let's see what would happen if you started with $100 and invested *another* $100 every year.

Year 1:	Year 5:	Year 10:	Year 25:	Year 50:
$110	$832.61	$2,012.49	$11,901.65	$139,769.02

You notice what happened? After ten years (and $1,000 invested you doubled your money—just by placing it in the investment! Plus, you ended up over $130,000 richer. Granted, over 50 years, you invested a total of $5,000, but that's chump change compared to what you end up with.

And what would happen if your growth rate was only 2 percent bigger? Say 12 percent?

Again, you've invested only $5,000 in total, but if your investments earn a 12 percent return instead of 10 percent, you'll have nearly $300,000 someday.

So where is all this extra money coming from? To put it simply, when you invest that $100, someone somewhere is borrowing it from you. And *you* are charging *them* compounding interest for the privilege.

Year 1:	Year 5:	Year 10:	Year 25:	Year 50:
$112	$887.75	$2,276.04	$16,633.40	$297,702.26

TAKING STOCK OF STOCKS

Sometimes you just want to have a little fun with your money now. That's why a lot of people buy company shares of stock—just a fancy name for a tiny piece of a business. By owning a slice of a company that sells something you love, you can have a lot of fun researching it and following how the company is doing. You can follow the news in business sections of newspapers, online, or on TV.

Did your company just announce a cool new product? Watch your money grow. Did their factory just burn down? Watch out! That's going to cost you, too.

Time is on *your* side

Time might heal all wounds, but as the charts show it is also one of the most important ingredients to investment success. And that's why your age makes you an incredibly powerful force. Because you have so much time to let your investments grow, you can start out with only enough money to buy a new outfit and end up with enough to take a trip to Disneyland, or wait a little longer and buy a house! (Okay, you'll be taking your own kids or grandkids to the theme park, but still...)

Beware the dark side

Does everything here sound a little too good to be true? Can't believe that investing would be that simple? Or reliable? Well, okay, you're right, it's not. Just as you need to tend to a plant to make sure it's growing well, you need to check in on your investments and make changes from time to time.

That's because not every investment is going to follow a straight line like the ones shown here. Like gardening, some investing years are better than others. One year there might be bright sun and ample rain, so your plant grows tall. The next year? A plague of locusts turns a whole garden into a chomped-up mess—and everybody's plants are leveled to the ground.

The same idea applies to investing. You buy stock from Busy Bee Honey Co., and for the first two years you're making some sweet cash. But look out! Thousands of bees get sick one year and die. Suddenly the company stock isn't worth as much anymore because there's less chance the business will be profitable. Your investment loses money.

Diversify!

So how can you protect that money? Here's one way: Diversify your investments. That's just a complicated way to say, "Don't put all your eggs in one basket," and in many cases, the system works. Good investors know that if they put some of their money in company stocks close to home, some in international stocks, and then invest in gold, too (just as an example), at least a couple of those investments will probably make enough money to pick up the slack if the third one tanks. Remember mutual funds? They're based on the same idea.

Other people protect their money from big dips by investing only in companies that are pretty safe bets. They're usually big, well-known corporations that show steady profits year over year. These investments typically don't make a ton of money, but they rarely lose a huge amount.

Why do we pay taxes?

Congratulations! You just got your very first paycheck for putting in two weeks at the local hockey arena selling chips and hotdogs. You've been dreaming about this day since you took the job—and know exactly how much cash you'll be taking to the bank. So you open the envelope and...what's this?! Hey! Who took a chunk of your money? Relax. That's called paying taxes. It's something everyone eventually shells out for somehow through income or sales tax.

A tax is money the government collects from its citizens to pay for public schools, safe highways, clean water, garbage collection, prisons, hospitals, and other services. But why do these things need to be paid using tax money? Why can't we just pay for what we use instead? Simple. No one person (unless you were wildly rich) would be able to afford it. By pooling all our money together, though, governments can.

Tax systems around the world, including those in North America, are subject to a lot of debate, but they are generally based on our ability to pay. The richer you are, the more tax you can afford to pay. If you are making very little, however, you pay less.

No one likes to pay taxes, but everybody has to. Even you. (Hey, think of it as a sign of maturity. Now you can grumble about taxes along with your parents!)

Follow the wiggly line

Just know that history has shown us that even as investments go down over the course of days, weeks, and years, sometimes they eventually gain value and climb again—and investors make their money back. That is, if they are able to wait around long enough for the swing back up. Even after something as disastrous as the Great Depression, the markets eventually rebounded and it was back to "buy low and sell high" all over again.

But sometimes an investment loses money for a long time or never recovers. A public company goes bankrupt. A mining business never hits gold. For a lot of people (including me), it's really hard to know when to sell an investment or when to hold on a little longer and see if it starts making money again.

It's worrisome stuff, especially if you were planning on using that money soon. How would you like it if you invested $20 in your friend's fishing bait-and-tackle business (We DIG Worms!™), hoping to use the profits next month to buy a baseball ticket, and your enterprising buddy decided he hated dirt? You paid for his shovels and plastic containers, thinking he would both pay you back and give you a cut of the profits. Then nothing. Good-bye, ballgame.

Going public

When a private company slices itself up and offers those pieces to the public to buy. Yes, if you own stock in a company, you really do own a piece of it, you old moneybags.

So why am I investing again?

Knowing investments can lose big money, maybe you're wondering why anyone bothers with them. Easy. A lot of the time investing pays off and people end up with more money than they started with.

One more thing. Knowing what you know now, are you interested in investing? You'll have to get your parents to help you, since kids aren't actually allowed to own stock, including mutual funds and some types of bonds. In many places you have to wait until you turn 18 before investments can be in your own name.

In the meantime, you can open a bank account or just plunk a jar on your desk and throw 10 percent of all the money that comes your way into it. Use the time to learn as much as you can about investing. Read newspapers, visit online sites, or talk to some people who know their stuff.

Bull Market and Bear Market

When things are sunny on the money front for everyone, we say we're experiencing a bull market. But when stocks take a nosedive and no one wants to buy, that's a bear market. You've got to wonder, though. Why pick a bull to represent happy times? Wouldn't it be easier to remember the term if we called it a fluffy bunny market or sweet kitten market? I'm just saying...

Meet an Expert!
Amanda Mills,
Loose Change, Canada

What the heck is a financial therapist? Ask Amanda Mills. She's the founder of Loose Change in Toronto and one of the few people on the planet who listens to people talk about their money emotions for a living.

Often people will come to her when they're feeling stressed or anxious about how they handle their cash. Some clients go on huge shopping sprees and can't figure out why they're drowning in debt. Other people visit Amanda, who also happens to be an accountant, because they hoard their money and are terrified to spend it. Amanda's job is to listen and then help them figure out why they feel the way they do about money. Remember we said that money is never just about money? That money also influences feelings? Amanda believes that, too.

"Silence is at the root of a lot of the problems we have with money," she says, mentioning that because a lot of parents don't talk about money—things like how they earn or invest it—a lot of kids grow up feeling stupid about money. So they make a lot of mistakes when they grow up.

Is it time to break the cycle in your house?

"One of the most important things that kids can do with their parents is to urge them to teach and talk about money," she says.

Amanda admits her own family didn't chat about earning, spending, or saving much when she was a girl. But now that she has a job that allows her to talk about money all day long, she's inspired.

"I love how real these conversations are. When people talk frankly about money, there's no bull. If you really understand how the money works, you can understand a lot about a person," she says.

AMANDA'S 3 TIPS TO START SAVING

1. Get yourself a goal

So that unbearably cool skateboard is calling your name. Just think about all those totally awesome ollies and kickflips... Guess what? It looks like you've got yourself a financial goal there, dude. Amanda says that if you pick something that you really, really want, you'll have an easier time saving for it because other things you could spend your money on will seem like a waste. Instead, keep your eye on the prize.

2. Take yourself seriously

In other words, grab your parents and go meet your bank manager. You might be a kid now, but you're also a future customer. Or ask your mom or dad to teach you how to look at your bank account online so you can keep tabs on how fast your money is growing. The point is, if you give your money more than a passing thought, you can build the skills you need to save up for things you want. (And yes, you can still splurge on music, candy, or a night at the movies with friends. Who wants to be a miser?)

3. Pay up, Pops!

"If your parents aren't paying you an allowance, they're really cheating you. They're controlling all of the money decisions, and that's not fair," says Amanda. (Don't you wish she were your favorite aunt or something? Me, too.) She has a point. Even if your parents can afford only 50 cents a week, it's important that you learn how to spend and save your money responsibly. Learning what to do with your allowance now will teach you how to handle your salary in the future. So negotiate an allowance and open a bank account.

Saving up for the big stuff

Save money, good. Spend every cent, bad. It's not rocket science, right? So why, despite having all this evidence, do so many of us drag our heels when it comes to saving ? Lots of reasons, really. We worry we're going to make bad investment choices, or think we don't understand enough about investing in the first place. And sometimes we simply don't have any money to invest. Not much you can do about that one.

But there's one other giant reason that keeps a lot of people from spending money to make money. It's called inertia. Huh?

Ever tried to push a train? Right—it's heavy and takes forever to get moving. It's "inert." But if you stick with it and get that train going, it becomes next to impossible to stop. That force is called momentum.

In a way, learning to save and invest is the same thing. If you don't put any effort into it, inertia rules and you go nowhere. But stick with it and build up some momentum, and your savings can really fly.

The case for doing something

Before you go to bed at night, chances are some grown-up asks you if you've done your homework. Oops! But instead of cracking open the books, you brush your teeth and hit the hay with a sinking feeling in the pit of your tummy.

So what happened? You froze. The task just seemed so big, you did nothing.

But some scientists have found that the secret to happiness is kicking fear, worry, and plain old inertia to the curb and doing something—anything!

There's just one problem—humans may be hard-wired for laziness. If given a choice, we're more likely to take the easy path in order to save energy. And that's exactly what researchers discovered when they asked a bunch of students to fill in a survey and then walk to one of two locations to hand it in. One station was close, the other far away. It turned out that the students who took a hike said they felt happier than the ones who wussed out.

So do something. Build some momentum. Not only will your savings thank you, but you'll feel pretty good about it.

The case for doing nothing

That said, if we know that we're a lazy bunch, why not use this trait and turn it into a good thing?

As it turns out, some companies are doing just that—and their employees are getting to save money without even thinking about it. That's because researchers discovered that even though a lot of companies give their workers the option to save some of their paycheck every month in an investment, a third of the employees can't be bothered. Or they forget to sign up.

So they tried another approach. The researchers looked at what happened when companies automatically signed up every new employee and *made them save*. If people wanted out, they'd have to fill out a pesky form. But it seems even that simple task was too much hassle. In the end, 96 percent of the workers were stockpiling money in an investment every month because it was easier than opting out.

It looks like there's something to be said for laziness. At least sometimes.

Psst! Here's one more reason to save money and dream about your exciting future: Happier people make the world a better place. See Chapter 9 to find out how...

KIRA EXPLAINS: "Saving" the World!

HOW SAVING FOR A RAINY DAY CAN MEAN SUNNY DAYS AHEAD ON THE OTHER SIDE OF THE PLANET.

"Can I really save enough money in less than three years to take a trip around the world with my family?"

Meet Sophia and Simon. For as long as they can remember, they and their parents have been into travel. They've taken trips to Rome, the British Virgin Islands, and closer to home, too. But then...their mom and dad hatch a plan.

But how? Sophia and Simon's parents aren't rich. They're teachers. The family sits down for a long talk.

Soon the kids make a list of places they want to visit. They research airfare while their parents look into the cost of food and safe accommodation. Their savings goal: $60,000.

Now they've got to make that money. So they have a big garage sale, Sophia babysits, Simon cuts grass for neighbors, and Mom teaches summer school.

They read the business section of their newspaper, see how their fave companies are doing... and invest. Watch that money grow!

It's not always easy to pull back on spending. No restaurant meals and no splurges at the mall. Sometimes it seems other kids are having more fun.

Then the stock market takes a hit and Dad doesn't seem so chipper either... until the investments bounce back.

Two years later... they get the final OK from schools and work, pack their bags, and hop on a plane. In no time flat, they're world travelers.

After they come home, Sophia and Simon write a book about what they saw. They also charge $150 a pop to speak at schools. Soon they raise enough money to start saving for the next trip!

> *"Money won't create success, the freedom to make it will."*
>
> – NELSON MANDELA

CHAPTER NINE

CAN YOU SPARE A DIME?

Why poverty gets a poor grade.

Q: WHY DO WE CALL MONEY DOUGH?

A: Because everyone in the world *kneads* it.

All right, bad joke. Because for a lot of people, finding money to pay for a loaf of bread, shoes that fit, and a comfortable bed is no laughing matter. In fact, for over half of the world's population, these are major luxuries. These are people who live in what the World Bank calls "moderate poverty." That means living on less than $2 a day.

Two bucks? That's peanuts!

Even when you factor in countries' different currency rates and standards of living, $2 isn't much at all. In some areas of the world it would (barely) cover the cost of a pack of stickers.

Around the world $1 (U.S.) might buy:

- In Brazil: one-tenth of a pizza

- In Germany: a one-way bus ticket

- In Kenya: eight cups of milk

- In Mexico: two kids' passes to see a Mayan pyramid

- In South Korea: one DVD rental

- In the Philippines: four-fifths of a Big Mac

Even in countries struggling with poverty, $2 just doesn't go very far. Chances are your family eats more than a bit of pizza or a couple of burgers each day, right?

Are you wondering what causes some people to be rich and others poor? Before we try to answer that question, let's talk about what poverty actually *is*.

But my best friend has a new TV...

How do we define poverty? That's a big, complex question that lots of economists and social scientists have tried to tackle over the years. But there's one person who did a pretty good job of giving it a whirl way back in the 1770s. He was a classical economist from Scotland named Adam Smith. His theory? Poverty was the lack of basic necessities of life. He called them "necessaries."

Is this *really* necessary?

Every society has an absolute minimum standard of living that includes things like shelter, food, clean water, and clothes. Everything a person needs to stay alive. That's a given, right? But according to Smith, even if you had all those things, you would still be considered poor if you didn't also have some extra items that your society thinks you need to be considered "decent." In Smith's day, he said everyone should have a linen shirt and a pair of leather shoes. If you didn't own them, people would know you were poor.

"Basket of Goods" approach
The more things you have in your basket, the less likely you are to be considered poor.

Smith's conclusion: It's these extras that help us go through life with dignity and without shame.

What was so neat about his definition was that is took *location* into account. He said that the "custom of the country" would dictate what the extra items would be. So say you live in the U.S. Having a pair of running shoes for gym class is pretty important. Without them, other kids in your class would likely notice and you'd probably feel uncomfortable when your teacher asked you *again* why you didn't have them. At the same time, if you lived in India, where 27 percent of the population lives on less than $1 a day, going to school without your sneakers probably wouldn't raise anyone's eyebrow. The customs of each country are different.

We now call this the "basket of goods" approach. The more things you have in your basket, the less likely you are to be considered poor.

Is a cellphone an extra?

There, you just did it. Did what? By asking that question, you've just revealed the main problem with Smith's definition. Because much of poverty is defined by a society's extras, it leaves the door wide open for debate. That's why you'll find economic experts duking it out over whether a cellphone is required to live fully in our society today or something that is just nice to have. In other words, we have to ask ourselves what specific things, and how much of them, we need. A nice apartment? One sofa? Three beds? Two cars? Six pairs of jeans? Where do we draw the line?

115

In some ways, that line's location depends on how we see the world. Anti-poverty advocates tend to include more items in their list of must-haves, while pro-business folks take the stance that, for example, a television is an amenity (i.e., a luxury), not a necessity.

So what would you include in your poverty basket? Take a minute and think about it. Chances are, it will be different from your friends' baskets.

Rich? Poor? Doing okay?

Not everybody uses the basket approach when dividing rich from poor. In Europe, some organizations figure it out another way: If you have less than 60 percent of what the average person makes, you're considered poor. (It's a little more complicated than that. The experts throw around words like "median income" and "income distribution," but this is the basic idea.)

In the U.S. and Canada, experts come up with an absolute, specific number known as the poverty line. For instance, in 2008 the poverty line in the U.S. was pegged at $29.58 a day for a single adult under the age of 65. Many European experts find this thinking a little weird—after all, can you really say someone is poor if he makes $29.57 a day, but that the same person would be doing okay if making $29.59?

What's fair, or even logical, about that?

Why go only halfway?

Have you ever heard about the fight for equality for women in the workplace? Ever wondered just how that was going? Here's the (raw) deal: In a lot of countries, school is still not promoted for girls. Women in these places often end up working out of their homes or in other informal—or even dangerous—settings. The pay is lousy, and forget about benefits like sick leave or paid breaks: They don't exist.

With so many women either toiling away at crummy jobs or not working at all, whole countries suffer. Think about it. What would happen if half a nation's population ditched their lousy jobs and went to university instead? And what would happen if those college grads then landed awesome jobs bringing in the bigger money? There would be new thinkers, new dreams, and new ideas flying all over the place. People would have more money to spend in their nation's economy, too. Education is power and entire families and countries would benefit.

Many politicians, journalists, and researchers say opening up the whole world to all women is possibly the single best way to make life better in developing nations.

And while we're on *that* topic...

Let's pretend it's Saturday. Allowance day! And now you're going to take some of your cash down to the corner store and spend it on a Choco-Dreambar 2000. But wait! There's something you've got to know before you take your first bite. Sorry to break this to you, but that cocoa is loco. It's gone bad, but not in the way you'd expect.

The thing is, in order to harvest the cocoa beans for much of the world's chocolate, thousands of people—even kids—toil for little or no money. Think hot sun, dangerous tools, exposure to chemical pesticides, and walking long hours in the grueling heat. And...these kids are so busy working, they can't go to school.

Who needs school anyway?

Everybody—if they want to stop poverty cold and live a happier, better life. Even though it seems like ditching school and hitting the job market to make some fast money would be a great idea, it's not. Because as this cocoa story shows, work isn't always a good thing if people are forced to take on icky, abusive, or dangerous jobs that make them feel sick or sad.

Think this only happens in other countries? Think again. We see a similar situation play out closer to home when people work at low-paying jobs that are like personal one-way tickets to Nowhereville.

Here's what I mean. Let's say your favorite auntie, Lisa, is making just a little over minimum wage at a job that's boring and repetitive. It's just barely enough to pay for rent, food, and clothes for her family. So she asks for more shifts so she can make more cash. Only one problem with that: She really wants to go back to school so she can gain more skills and get a better job—but now that she's working so many hours, there's just not enough time. Before you know it, your fave family member is caught in a nasty cycle that keeps her from eventually finding a great job and kicking poverty to the curb.

Think of it this way. Working for money should make our lives better, not worse, right?

So sure, it's easy to take school for granted—or hate it, even—when our government offers it for free. But don't forget, many countries around the world either expect families to fork over money so their kids can get an education, or offer few schools in poor, rural areas. This is a big drag because a lot of families who live there tell us they would send their kids to school if they could. They know that school = jobs = no more poverty.

Rich Country, Broke Country

You're right. It isn't fair. We live in a world where inequality rules the day. Depending on where you woke up this morning, you might snarfle down a bowl of cereal and then grab a banana on the way to school—or crawl out from under a blanket on the street and dig around for something to eat for your little brother.

How did this happen? Why do some countries, and the people who live in them, seem to need more financial help than others? This is not an easy question to answer, but there are some reasons that seem to pop up.

History

It's hard to stop being poor if you've been poor a long time. Poverty usually builds up over many years, so don't expect to squash it in a few short weeks, months, or even years.

Geography

Countries that are located closer to richer countries often do better than ones that are separated from them. That's not always the case—Mexico shares a border with the United States, but struggles with poverty.

Natural resources

Countries swimming in water, minerals, or lumber usually become rich. But sometimes natural resources hurt. Diamonds and oil can spark fights and even wars.

Food dumping

Free food! Good idea, right? Some experts caution that if rich countries send food aid to poor countries when it's no longer an emergency, local farmers can't compete with the prices and are driven out of jobs.

Bad systems

In some parts of Africa, a quarter of crops rot before anybody can eat them! The technology systems might be bad, and there can be insect infestations, mold growth, or other damage due to heat and humidity.

War

Looking for a sure-fire way to bankrupt a nation? Go to war for a long time. The more money that goes to feeding the war machine, the less there is for schools, medical care, and other things that make life safe and fun.

Bad economy

Sometimes the economy tanks and people start losing their jobs. If enough of them get fired or laid off, they can't pay for stuff. If they can't pay, other people lose their jobs. The cycle continues...

Corruption

Some people in political power are only looking out for Number One. They use money that should be going to their people to line their own pockets. The powerful get rich and the rest stay poor.

Doing the wrong thing

Sometimes the country itself isn't to blame for a person's dire financial situation. In some cases, people are simply bad at handling their money, no matter where they live.

No girls allowed

Many nations allow only men to work. That means about 50 percent of a country's smart, talented people aren't able to contribute great things.

Turn down the heat

Looking for one more reason that poor countries tend to stay that way? Sometimes poverty has nothing to do with school, jobs, politics, or anything else people can actually change. That's right. I'm talking about the weather.

Historically, hot countries are poorer than cold countries. Tropical weather creates perfect conditions for diseases such as malaria, little parasites in drinking water, and leprosy. Sick people can't work, so productivity (the amount of work people do) plummets. The hope is that as medical technology grows, more people will feel like a million bucks. Take Singapore. Even though it's often hot there, it's considered a very productive country today.

Here's where you come in

Great news. Passionate grown-ups and kids all around the world are coming up with new ways to do good and feel good, too. We're volunteering to teach villagers in Ghana new ways to keep garbage away from source water to make it safe to drink. We're building websites that with a click of a button make it easy for anyone with a computer to raise money and buy food and medicine for others who are hungry or ill. Some kids are even creating their own charities.

And the rest of us? We're taking a few moments out of our day and donating money.

I'VE GOT A BONE TO PICK...

And it has to do with the word "poor." I'll tell you, I much prefer the word "broke" instead. Because think about it. "Poor" has an unbelievable amount of baggage attached to it. Call somebody poor and you're telling them they are less than someone else.

That's not fair. Maybe the person is an amazing singer or can do funky things with her thumbs. Maybe he's the smartest kid in the school or an incredible athlete. But call someone "poor" and you're not seeing the whole person. Call them "broke" instead? Then it's just about the money, honey.

Broke is a state of being. Poor is a state of mind.

That's my two cents.

Here, I got this gift for you

Here's one awesome reason to give away money instead of keeping it all to ourselves: Giving makes us feel good. Hey, our spit doesn't lie.

Huh? Spit?

Seriously. A few years ago, Elizabeth Dunn, a psychology professor at the University of British Columbia who studies money and happiness, came up with an experiment that went something like this: She had a class play "the dictator game." Some students, the "dictators," were given $10 in coins and paired up with other students. Then they were given a choice: How much of their money would they give to their partner? (Remember, this was real money they could keep after the game was over.) Some people gave away all their money. Some people gave away nothing. Most fell somewhere in between.

As it turns out, the more money people gave away, the happier they ranked themselves later.

After the game was over, the students also put a piece of special cotton, called Salivette, in their mouths to offer spit samples. The saliva results confirmed everything. People who kept more of the money for themselves felt more shame. And the more shame they felt, the higher their stress hormones.

"It was kind of fun because we can see these effects turning up not only in their emotion ratings, but also in their saliva," says Elizabeth now.

Another day, she sent her assistants to give $5 and $20 bills to strangers. Half of the strangers were told to spend the money on themselves; the other half had to spend it on others. When the results came back, the researchers learned that, again, people who spend "pro-socially" (in other words, on gifts or charities) are a happier bunch.

But what causes the bliss? Does giving really make us happy, or are generous people simply more joyful? It's hard to say, admits Elizabeth, although the results from some of her experiments suggest that people definitely get a happiness boost from giving.

"Either way, we see that happiness and spending on others seem to like to hang out together," she says.

Do-gooders R Us

Want to take the concept of giving even further? Jump in! Get involved! Make a difference! All the people who work and volunteer at these cool charitable organizations do.

They've got disease covered...

Bzzz. Slap. Darned skitters! For many of us, mosquitoes are a summer nuisance. But for others, they can be deadly. Malaria, a disease some mosquitoes carry, actually kills nearly a million grown-ups and kids each year. The United Nations launched a campaign called Nothing But Nets in 2006 to get people donating money for nets that hang around people's beds to keep them safe from the blood-hungry, disease-carrying buzzers. Hello, net. Good-bye, mosquito.

They're cleaning up the environment...

After watching the movie *An Inconvenient Truth*, 12-year-old Alec Loorz from California wanted to give other kids the scoop about global warming. Now, a few years later, his organization, Kids vs. Global Warming, spreads the word and shows people how to recycle, plant trees, grow their own food, and travel using their body's own power.

Five bur
question:
for Elizabeth,
money expert

WANT TO KNOW HOW PEOPLE SHOULD SPEND THEIR CASH TO FEEL GREAT? I DID, TOO, SO I CALLED UP ELIZABETH DUNN, A SAVVY EXPERIMENTAL RESEARCHER IN VANCOUVER, CANADA, WHO IS ALSO AN AWARD-WINNING TEACHER.

Q Studying the way people deal with their money is interesting. Is this what you always wanted to do when you grew up?

A Actually I wanted to be an actress! I kind of get to be one, though, because I get up on stage and talk to big groups of people about my work now.

Q What's the most surprising thing you've learned about feelings and money?

A Money doesn't seem to provide as much happiness as people expect. So instead of focusing on how much we're going to earn, maybe the best thing people can do is to think more carefully about how they're going to spend what they've got.

Q Okay, so knowing what you know now about money and happiness, let's say somebody gave you $20,000. What would you do with it?

A I would definitely use a lot of it to benefit other people. I would also try to use it to have some neat experiences that I might not otherwise get. (Research shows that spending money on experiences, like riding horses or going skiing, makes us happier than buying things.) And I would treat myself to little pleasures and keep a stock of money set aside to pay for them.

Q Would you save any of it?

A Well...I guess so.

Q It wouldn't make you happy?

A That depends on what I would eventually spend it on!

They're ramping up reading...

Want to unload a few books you no longer read? Just look for a Reading Tree bin near you and dump them in. Reading Tree takes books that might end up in the landfill and gets them into the hands of readers all over the United States and Canada. Book too beat up to read? No worries. The organization also recycles them.

They're giving animals new life...

Swooping through the night sky and making skin prickle all over the world. Why the heck do we need to save the bat? Bat Conservation International in Texas says bats are wildly misunderstood little critters that are important to our ecosystems. Leaving the flying insect annihilators to fend for themselves is just batty.

They're helping kids every day...

All work and no play? No way! Right to Play, an organization that started in Toronto, gets over 700,000 children around the world jumping, hopping, and playing sports. For kids who have been stuck in war-torn areas or turned into child workers, it's the first time they've ever had a chance to just be kids.

MIRROR, MIRROR ON THE WALL. WHO ARE THE MOST GENEROUS OF THEM ALL?

When it comes to giving money away, people in the U.K. seem to have their wallets open more than anyone else. A little more than eight out of ten Brits give to charity. Canada comes second, with 77 percent of Canadians saying they sign away some cash each year. Other interesting results:

Forty-nine percent of Americans say they think animal charities are the most worthy cause.

In India, donators are most passionate about keeping kids healthy and happy.

The Swiss are most worried about fighting climate change.

(Source: UnLtdWorld)

Bringing in the BIG money

Sometimes individual charities, foundations, and organizations aren't enough. Remember when we talked about the causes of poverty a few pages back? Sometimes entire countries are so broke and broken, they need lots of outside help. That's where organizations like the World Bank and the International Monetary Fund come in.

What does the World Bank do?

Let's answer that with a little history lesson: The World Bank was launched in 1944 at the tail end of the Second World War. At first, it was meant to give devastated countries money to rebuild their war-ravaged cities and to get their economy back on its feet again. France—a nation that was particularly ruined by German occupation and numerous battles—was the first country to use the money.

Since then, however, the World Bank has become less concerned with helping countries clean up after wars. Instead, it's more concerned with trying to slash poverty in the world's least developed areas. It gives out billions of dollars in loans and grants each year, and has brought clean water and electricity to millions of people. Most of its money comes from its own borrowing and from the 184 countries that are its members.

The upside and the downside

At first glance, this World Bank idea all seems pretty nifty. Sure enough, there are a lot of people who like what the World Bank is *supposed* to do...but don't like how they *actually* do it. Sometimes, it refuses to give money to corrupt countries that have dictators. That kind of makes sense. Why would you give money to someone who might turn around and keep it for himself and his evil buddies?

Here's the problem: Why does the Bank get to decide who is corrupt and who isn't? Also, some argue that withholding money hurts the people in that country—the ones who are really struggling—far more than the dictator. In addition, there's criticism that the interest the World Bank charges for its loans is too high for these countries to pay back. As a result, the countries just end up racking up even more

125

debt than they started with (and are now worse off than before). In the past few years, though, the World Bank has found ways to bring that interest rate down.

How about that International Monetary Fund?

Great question. A lot of people can't tell the difference between the two organizations. Both of them loan out money to countries in need. (Remember Bubbleland on pp. 84–85?) But the IMF is actually a little different than the World Bank. For starters, it loans money to any country that needs it. Iceland, for example, received money from the IMF when it faced a monumental credit crunch. IMF loans are intended to be short-term fixes so a country can get back on its feet again. The World Bank, however, is often in it for the long haul.

Charities that try to help people one dollar at a time. Billion-dollar loans from the World Bank and the IMF. But there's also another way to give everyone, no matter where they live, a chance to go from day-to-day survival to having enough money to live on and even plan for the future.

It's called microcredit. Read on to find out how it works!

Pass it on. So now that you have a good sense of what causes poverty and what charities do to help, want to find out how you can make a difference? Go to Chapter 10 and let's get cracking.

KIRA EXPLAINS: Microloans!

HOW $25 CAN GROW AND G-R-O-W... AND TURN A WHOLE VILLAGE AROUND

Can a tiny microloan make that much of a difference? Find out!

Say hi to Amolika. She lives in a small village in Bangladesh with her mom, dad, and two sisters. Her dad grows jute used to make burlap sacks, rope, twine, and mats. But now times are tough and there isn't even enough money to buy mangos at the market—or for the girls to go to school. That really bums Amolika out.

Then Amolika remembers something from school. There's a bank in the city that lends money to people with big dreams—and a plan. She tells her mom.

After meeting with a nice man who visits them at their home and answering many questions, Amolika's mother is given a small loan. "This is not free money. It's a loan, and it needs to be paid back."

Amolika loves to watch her mom weave, and soon Amolika's mom's mats are a hit. Everybody is asking her if she'll be back at the market next week.

Now Amolika and her mom are weaving mats every chance they get. Her dad wants to help the business, too, so he heads out to show larger stores some samples. He comes back with orders.

Now the family is so busy they have enough money to send the girls back to school— and hire people to weave mats. More men are working with Amolika's dad, too.

Now there's a shortage of men to do other jobs in town—so their pay goes up. Amolika has even more classmates to learn and play with!

By now the family business employs a lot of people. And because Amolika's mom paid the bank back, other banks are willing to lend her more money.

They build a factory and make more jobs! Stores open. Local businesses thrive. And Amolika? She's off to college to learn how to lend money to others with a dream and a plan!

"Don't make money your goal. Instead, pursue the things you love doing, and then do them so well that people can't take their eyes off you."

– MAYA ANGELOU

CHAPTER TEN

RAISE FUN
A LITTLE

Or should that be funds? Because making money to give away is a hoot when you do it with friends.

IT'S DEADLY, DANGEROUS, AND DOWNRIGHT DEPRESSING.
That's right, we're still talking poverty here. But before you flip to some other page looking for something a bit more uplifting, stop! I've got some great news.

You're about to find out all the cool things you can do with money to turn the world around. For just a few cents a day (as they like to say on TV), you can do your part to clean up your local river, send another kid to camp, give cancer a run for its money, and even feed a family of four this year. True, you might not have mega bucks to throw around and get your name engraved on the wall at a museum, yet there's plenty you can do to still have an impact and make your money count.

Kids just like you have been known to collect new shoes to give to other children who have never had a new pair in their lives. Others donate DVDs to hospitals, dish out Thanksgiving turkey in soup kitchens, or snuggle abandoned animals at the local animal shelter every week.

Fundraising. Volunteering. Charity. Stick them all together and you can make the world a happier place for everybody.

Calling all billionaires!

Guess what? While I was researching this page for this book, news broke out that nearly 40—count 'em, 40—American billionaires pledged to give away at least half of their fortunes to charity someday.

Star Wars creator George Lucas is on the list. So is Jeff Skoll, the past president of eBay. It happened because Microsoft head honcho Bill Gates and Warren Buffett, a famous investor, simply asked them to do it. ("Come on, you can spare a couple billion. Everybody's doing it...") By signing the "Giving Pledge," the ultra-wealthy promise to donate most of their wealth in their lifetimes or after they die.

If all the 400-plus American billionaires make the same vow, people around the world will feel the force—to the tune of $600 billion.

Calling all kids with an $8 allowance!
Okay, we can't all be billionaires. But you and I can use our personal power to do good in the world, too. You can:

- Write and sell a cookbook with your friends, produce a play at school and charge admission, record some music and sell the CD, or make up some other fundraiser for a charity you believe in.

- Start your *own* charity or non-profit (a non-profit is actually a lot easier to run, since it doesn't have so many rules to follow).

- Or how about creating a Giving Circle? You can do that, too. How? Keep on reading...

Wheel of fortune

Who wants to volunteer and raise money alone? Join or start a Giving Circle and do good with good friends. A Giving Circle is basically a group of people who get together to pool their time and money in order to have a bigger impact on the causes they want to get involved in.

Say you and your friends decide to support your local animal shelter. You can work together selling doggy treats for charity or meet up after school and do volunteer dog walking together.

Not only do Giving Circles tend to raise more money than a bunch of individual people donating separately, but they're also fun! To start one:

1. Ask your friends to join.

2. Decide what causes float your boat.

3. Research charities you want to support.

4. Plan fundraising events.

5. Have regular meetings.

6. Cha-ching! Hand over that well-deserved cash.

Build a school to build a life

Curious as to how far the money you raise could go? Remember how in Chapter 9 we were talking about the importance of education in wiping out poverty? This is kind of ambitious, but just for argument's sake: Imagine if you and your Giving Circle got together and raised enough money to build a school for rural kids in, say, the West African country of Sierra Leone. Let's take a peek...

Raise money through bake sales, car washes, dance-a-thons, and selling fair-trade chocolate bars. Stay focused, eyes on the prize, and over $10,000 later...

A crew of grown-ups and teens from your country work with local builders to build a new school. Your money also pays for desks, a blackboard, paper, and pencils.

Local kids finally have a chance to go to a free school!

The cocoa farmers still need workers, so unemployed parents and relatives take over the jobs at the cocoa plantations from those kids and bring in money for their families.

Meanwhile, kids are learning to read, write, and do math. Now that they have an education, a whole world opens up to them. UNICEF, a global children's charity and arm of the United Nations, claims that for every year of schooling a child gets, the amount of money she could earn goes up 10 percent.

Once these kids grow up and make a decent salary, their own children won't have to work either.

While there's no doubt that this is a grand dream, it goes to show that if planned out properly, a charitable mission can really pay off. Theoretically, all that bake sale money would have an impact on other kids, not just today, but way into the future, too. What a sweet deal!

Thinking you want to start a charity, too?

Take it from Marni across the page, starting a charity is a lot of hard work. Fortunately her mom and dad were able to help. But if you've got a great idea that can help the planet, and no one else has thought of it yet, building your own charity might make sense. Just remember:

- You may be too young to be president.
- You'll need to pull together a board of directors.

Meet the Experts!

Lexi, Romi, Marni, and Berni Marta,
Kid Flicks, United States

A private tour of Air Force One? That's what Marni and Berni Marta received in 2008 when the sisters won that year's President's Volunteer Service Award.

"My dad said, 'In my 50 years, I've never reached a point in my career when I've done something like this,'" says Marni now. "It just shows that you don't have to be a certain age to do something good."

That "something good" is Kid Flicks, a charitable organization that donates thousands of new and used movies on DVDs to children's hospitals across the U.S. and South Africa. Marni was just 11 years old when she and her three young sisters launched the project in 2002.

Not that they had any idea what they were getting themselves into. What started out as just a little spring cleaning at their home in California has since turned into a nationwide effort. Kid Flicks has donated over 56,600 DVDs for children and teens to over 566 hospitals and has helped thousands of kids pass the time while sick or recovering from surgery.

"I know when I'm in a bad mood I like to watch movies. I can only imagine how kids in the hospital are feeling," says Marni.

At first the sisters and their parents would drive from hospital to hospital to drop off the flicks, but after one grueling five-hour journey, they realized it was time to apply for grants and turn Kid Flicks into an official not-for-profit organization. Their dad, a lawyer, helped fill out the paperwork.

Even though the sisters are now scattered in cities across the country and are working or going to university, hardly a week goes by that they haven't received movie donations from kids, families, schools, churches, temples, groups, and even movie studios.

Some kids in other states even organize movie drives and collect DVDs for Kid Flicks.

"I think it's really empowering to see that age doesn't have to be an obstacle when it comes to doing something important for other people," Marni says.

KID FLICKS

- You'll have to apply to the government to get your charitable status (proof you're really a charity that can give donors tax receipts).

If you don't feel like jumping through so many hoops, consider volunteering at a similar organization that already exists. Then you can bring your great idea to them and maybe they'll run with it.

Put money where your brain is

Let's say you want to raise cash with friends to save the much-maligned giant moray eel. (The nine-foot sea monsters *are* kind of cute...if you squint and turn your head just so.) So you hop online and do your research. Soon you're reading about the Society of Eel Enthusiasts, a charity that researches all things *Gymnothorax javanicus* and helps preserve their natural habitat. Score.

Scam warning signs

Ring, ring! "Hello, would you like to donate money to the Blind Bat Firefighters' Foundation? We could really use your help." It seems like every night your family gets calls like this one, asking you to give, give, and give some more. But before your family donates a cent, ask yourself if the call makes sense.

- Con artists often use high-pressure tactics. It's okay to reject them. And it's okay to hang up.

- Fraudsters might thank you for a pledge you don't remember ever making. Then you feel trapped into donating again. Just say, "No way."

- Resist requests for cash. Legit charities take checks and credit cards. (But your mom and dad should never give their credit card number to anyone who calls out of the blue. They need to do their homework first.)

- Avoid charities that offer to send a courier or "runner" to your house to pick up your money.

- Pay close attention to charities that spring up overnight to tackle current events like floods or earthquakes. Real charities usually exist well before the worst happens.

- Trust your gut. If you have a funny feeling about the charity asking for your donation, go out and find another one you believe in.

But is this charitable organization worthy of your hard-earned money? After all, even though most charities and non-profits do good work, not all of them use their donors' money wisely. And some so-called charities are nothing but big, fat scammers ready to rake in a percentage of the billions of dollars nice people like you donate each year.

For instance, back in 2007, newspapers reported that the Wish Kids Foundation, which said it gave dying children their final wish, never actually helped anyone. Instead, the people who ran the fraudulent charity were really just trying to buy themselves an airplane!

So how can you tell the difference between legit charities and bogus ones?

First off, you'll want to do your homework. Governments and other organizations in the United States, Canada, and many other countries around the world offer lists of genuine charities online. You can also take a look at the charity's website. Many are required to tell people how their money is being spent. Some of it will go to fundraising, rent, staff wages, and bills. But most of it should go to its cause.

If you're having a tough time figuring out what the organization's annual report is telling you, ask your mom, dad, or a teacher to help you.

And don't feel bad about being nosy. If you're going to go to all the trouble of printing fundraising cookbooks or selling chocolates for a worthy cause with your friends, you need to know if your money is going to go to the right people and for the right reasons.

So where should my money go?

That's a really good question, and it's one only you can answer. Maybe your little sister has hydrocephalus (too much fluid around the brain), so you decide you want to give your allowance to a charity that helps kids with the condition. Or do you feel passionate about putting the brakes on global warming? There are many environmental organizations that do good work. Or maybe you really believe in the power of microlending and giving people a way to start their own business. Giving is partly an emotional process—and that's okay.

But here's something to think about. A few years ago something called the Copenhagen Consensus—a panel of eight super-smart economists (including three Nobel Prize winners)—figured out which causes would offer givers the most bang for their bucks.

Real rags to riches

(A.K.A. WHERE DO DONATED CLOTHES GO?)

So you've finally grown out of that mint-green sweater your grandma made you two birthdays ago (about time!) and you're ready to clean out the closet. Why not donate it to your local charity? The sweater will surely go to someone who really needs it (or at least has a penchant for mint-green cardigans), right?

Not so fast. A few years ago, ABC News in the U.S. decided to look a little closer at what happens to the many billions of pounds of clothing Americans donate to charity each year. What did the reporter discover? Your used clothes are usually sold rather than given away.

So let's say you decide to contribute the sweater to a good cause. What happens to it? Where does it go?

1 Usually, a small number of the best-quality castoffs get sold at a charity's thrift shop.

2 But if Gram's knitting doesn't make the grade, the sweater might join an estimated 90 percent of all clothing donations that get sold to textile-recycling firms. This doesn't sound too bad. The charity makes money by selling the clothes and the for-profit company does, too.

3 Even better, the recycler takes some of the unsellable clothes and turns them into cleaning cloths that people like mechanics use to wipe down car parts. Clothes, say good-bye to the dump.

4 But that sweater wasn't quite right for that purpose, so it gets loaded into a large crate and put on ships headed for developing countries.

5 Once in, say, Zambia, the clothing is unloaded and sold on the street at markets where people can buy cheap-quality clothes for a few bucks. Seems like a win-win? At this point a lot of people disagree about whether dumping cheap clothes on a community is a good or bad idea. What do you think?

THE UPSIDE
• Your old clothing creates new wealth for lots of people. The worker who loads the crate on the ship gets a job and so does the person who unloads it. Plus, people who don't have a lot of money get cheap clothes!
• Don't forget the environmental impact. Selling off used clothes keeps them out of landfills.
• The original charity you donated your clothes to will use the money it earns to help local people in need.

THE DOWNSIDE
• Because the market is flooded by cheap foreign clothes, many local clothing and textile industries go belly up, killing jobs and closing factories.
• Environmentally, it takes a lot of fuel to ship the clothes to the other side of the planet.
• The original charity sometimes receives very little money from selling your clothing to the company that ships it overseas. Or the charity is not actually a real charity at all, but a business that tries to pass itself off as a charity. Look out for scammers.

THE CONCLUSION?
Knowing all the angles, what's a kid to do with all that too-small attire collecting dust in the closet? Do your homework. Ask the charity that you plan to donate your garments to what it does with them, how much money it will actually make, and how it plans to spend it. Big name, well-known thrift stores are generally safe bets and will indeed use the majority of the money to help your community.

Best bets:

- Battling AIDS
- Giving healthy food to people who don't have enough
- Making trade between some counties easier
- Fighting malaria

Other good ideas:

- Wiping out malnutrition
- Giving more people the power to start their own businesses
- Making sure everyone has good drinking water

Although this list can give us an idea of what we need to focus on to help people live healthy, full lives, it is just a list. With your snazzy brainpower and drive to make a difference, don't be afraid to donate your time and money to causes that you believe in. It's your money, honey.

And *you* get to decide how it should be spent to make the world a better place.

We interrupt this chapter to bring you news about Hurricane Amy.

Who in their right mind would go to all the trouble of hosting a charity drive, collecting 2,000 pounds of clothes and canned food, and shipping it on planes to a country that has just been hit by an earthquake, hurricane, or flood, only to watch the donations molder and rust in crates for six months? But this story plays out more often than you'd think.

Surprised? Me, too. But it turns out there are some really good reasons why governments and relief agencies don't necessarily want your old jeans, shoes, and baked goods sent to ripped-to-shreds regions. Those donations just clog up the air and seaports and can actually make it harder to help the people who need it. Relief workers might lose valuable time sorting through boxes of goods when they could be out on the ground doing good. And sometimes clothes, food, and other things people send are not appropriate for the climate or culture they're being shipped to. It can be more cost effective to buy locally than to airlift goods from a faraway place.

But what if you still want to donate? One word of advice: Send money. Cash donations are quick, efficient, and can adapt to any culture, at any time. (In other words, they can't use your old snowsuit in Ghana, so give it to your little brother instead.)

Wow. You've come to the end of the last chapter. But not so fast! Flip the page and find out what you can do with that money wisdom now.

> *"Money, money, money*
> *Always sunny*
> *In the rich man's world."*
>
> – ABBA

THE END

Money is never just money

TALK ABOUT A GOOD LIFE. It's the first day of summer vacation. You're hanging out, floating on your diamond-encrusted inflatable alligator in your backyard wave pool, nestled beside your 36-bedroom mansion. Oh, and just for a little added fun, when you're not texting your friends, you're sipping some kind of fizzy drink and thinking, "Man, this is sweet. I've got it made in the shade."

(Insert finger snap here.)

Okay, let's take a quick detour back to reality, shall we?

No doubt about it, for most of us, life is a little more about digging around in our laundry baskets looking for a clean pair of socks than daydreaming by the pool. And I'm just going out on a limb here, but I bet you don't live in a mansion (although if you do, feel free to call me for lunch, dahling).

But here's the thing. If you're reading this book, there's a really good chance that you have at least one pair of shoes. And if you wanted to grab breakfast this morning? No problem. You just opened the refrigerator door or the pantry and swiped some cereal or at least a piece of fruit and a slice of last night's pizza. In other words, you've got enough cash to pay for life's necessities and necessaries.

A shocking confession!

The truth is you, me, and the kids in your school have got luck on our side. As a bunch of economists like to remind us, we're part of the top 2 percent of the world's population when it comes to opportunities and cash we have access to. In other words, the other 98 percent of the kids around the world have less money than we do.

But is it really that simple? We're lucky, so we have no money worries that keep us up at night? Of course not. Even though we know we've got it going on in the money department, let's not forget that it costs a lot of dough to live in developed countries. Maybe little two-bedroom bungalows on your street are being sold for $750,000 right now. That's the reality in some large cities around the world. Or that bag of potato chips in your hand? What did that set you back? A buck and a half? When I was a kid (which really wasn't all that long ago...), I'd plunk down a quarter for a bag of some sour-cream-and-onion goodness.

The point is, the value of money is always changing, and no matter where you live in the world, that can stress you out. How much money do you need to live on? What would happen to you if your dad lost his job? Everybody else in the class seems to get $5 a week for allowance and you only get $2. How does that make you feel about your parents—and yourself?

Does money have a lot of power over our brains? Absolutely. When we feel we don't understand how it works (what's compound interest again?), it's easy to get sucked into...

The Money Vortex of Fear!

Guess what? Simply by reading this book, you've put yourself on the path to understanding money, respecting money, and feeling good about money. You've probably got a better handle on why people make what they make and how to raise cash and donate to world problems you want to change. Maybe you've done the math and now understand exactly how much money you need to save up to be a millionaire someday.

You're like a superhero, you know. You've got power over money instead of feeling vulnerable or powerless. Money doesn't control you. You control money.

But what else can I do to feel the power?

Actually, you can do a lot. And although it's easy to feel a little guilty about your good fortune, don't! Seriously. Instead, look at it this way: You've got the chance to turn your incredible luck into action and make the world a better place.

Imagine...what would happen if U.S. kids took 10 percent of the $51 billion (a little over $5 billion) they spent on clothes, music, snacks, and entertainment in one year and used it to do some good for people, the environment, or the oft-forgotten pink fairy armadillo? (Nope, I didn't make that last one up. The little critters do exist.) Five billion dollars is said to be enough money to teach every kid and grown-up on the planet how to read.

Or imagine...a world where people spend only the money they make, and their trillion-dollar consumer debt is kicked to the curb.

Yup, you have the power to use money that builds eco-friendly cars, free schools in Nigeria, and chocolate bars that not only taste delish but are also created by people who are getting paid real money for the work.

Because remember, money is never just money, right? And now that you know it, too, spread the word. Tell your friends! Tell your grandma! Tell your math teacher! Who knows? Maybe you'll use all this newfound money wisdom to launch the first Nigerian Chocolate Eco-School Bus™. Hey, stranger things have happened.

GIMME MORE!

Has all this talk about money got you revved up hotter than a racecar's engine on a sweltering summer day? Cool. There are so many ways to learn more about money matters. And because you asked so nicely, I'll tell you what they are:

• Read books about money (like this one)

• Check out money websites and blogs

• Watch money shows on TV

• Read the business news in the paper

• Talk to your parents, teachers, and other cash-savvy folks

• Start an investment group with your friends and learn together

And guess what? If you pull it off, I'll be the first in line to buy a ticket and take a ride. You can put money on it...

So what do you think? Do you really need to be worrying about stocks, bonds, income tax, student loans, and mortgages now? Of course not! Now that you've read about those terms and know what they mean (and what they mean to your life), you'll do a lot less worrying about money and have a lot more fun with it instead.

So get out there and become an entrepreneur, form a money club with your friends and follow the stock market, or simply pick up an awesome shirt at a cut-rate price. Being smart about money is going to give you tons of confidence in other areas of your life, too.

Because now you know the truth about how much power money has and you've harnessed its high-wattage energy.

And the secret life of money? It's not so secret anymore.

Want to brush up on some more money info? The glossary starts on the next page. There's an index, too.

Coin That Phrase

ABM or ATM card
A bank card that lets you get at your money through the bank machine. Bank tellers often ask to see it, too. By the way, ABM and ATM stand for automated banking or teller machine.

Balance
The amount of cash you're storing in your bank account.

Bank
This is a business that's in the business of storing money for customers, giving loans and house mortgages, investing money, and offering other money services.

Bond
It's a loan you give with the understanding that the borrower will pay it back with interest on a certain date. Governments and companies offer bonds.

Bull market and bear market
When things are sunny on the money front for everyone, we say we're experiencing a bull market. But when stocks take a nosedive and no one want to buy, that's a bear market.

Collateral
What do you call a house, a car, or any other property? If you're a lender of money, you'd call that collateral. People who borrow money promise to hand over their collateral if they can't pay back the loan for some reason.

Credit
Simple stuff. Credit is loaned money that you've got to pay back. You usually pay a fee to borrow it.

Credit limit
How much loaned money can you get your hands on? That amount is called your credit limit.

Currency
Any kind of money (including shells, beans, you name it) that lots of people deem valuable and use as a medium of exchange.

Debt
Owe money and need to pay it back? You're in debt.

Default
Can't pay back the money you borrowed? We call that defaulting on a loan.

Depression
This is a word economists (and the rest of us) use to describe a period of time when there's super-high unemployment, so no one has money to buy much. And if no one is buying, more jobs go bust. A depression (or recession—its less intense cousin) is a hard cycle to break.

Direct deposit
Who needs a paper paycheck when your employer is willing to deposit it in your bank account automatically?

Dividend
As a shareholder, if your investment made a profit, your dividend is the money you'll get.

Euro
Ciao. You're in Italy (or Austria, Belgium, Finland, France, Portugal, Spain, Ireland, or many other European countries) and you want to buy an ice cream. Hand over the Euro. That's because back in 1999, a whole bunch of countries, or members of the European Union, decided to use a common currency that would replace their individual currencies. It made traveling and exporting easier.

Exchange rate
Why is the U.S. dollar said to be worth, say, £0.619 today and £0.620 tomorrow? We're talking about the exchange rate between the U.S. and the U.K. This rate is the value of a nation's currency when compared to another one.

Export
Selling goods and services to other people in other countries.

Federal Reserve
The central bank of the United States.

Going public
When a private company slices itself up and offers those pieces to the public to buy. Yes, if you own stock in a company, you really do own a piece of it.

Goods
Real things your can see and touch. Think cars, mouthwash, backpacks, and laptop computers.

Income
The money people get from wages, salary, investments, profits, and other sources.

Inflation
Inflation happens when there's too much money in circulation. In other words, because lots of people have lots of money, the value of things starts to drop. Sellers can jack up their prices—and buyers will still pay. Historically, inflation has averaged about 3 percent each year, so something that cost you $10 last year will cost $10.30 this year.

Interest
Want a loan? You've got to pay for it. Interest is the money someone shells out to borrow money, or the money a bank pays you when you have funds in your account.

Invest
Want to invest? No problem. Simply risk your money and time and hope you'll get something bigger and better back in return someday.

Miser
He's stingy, hoards money, and lives so frugally he eats tins of cheap tuna by the caseload. Misers can't stand to spend their money and prefer to hold on to it at all costs.

Mutual fund
A whole bunch of stocks and bonds together. The theory is if you buy a mutual fund, you won't be sinking all of your money into one company. You spread the joy (and the risk) around. If one of the companies tanks, the others will hopefully still be doing okay, so you won't lose as much.

National debt
The amount of money a whole country's government owes. For instance, as of July 15, 2011, the U.S. national debt was an astounding $14,348,863,605,350.75

Portfolio
Your collection of investments, such as stocks, bonds, or money in your bank account.

Profit
The money you make after your pay all your expenses.

Services
This is work people do that other people pay for. Think waiters, accountants, writers....

Start-up costs
Money entrepreneurs spend to start a business.

Stock
A share of stock is actually a piece of a company. If you own shares in a popular toy company and they release a new game everybody wants, the company will make more money—and so will you!

Stockholder or shareholder
If you buy stocks—a piece of a company—that would make you a stockholder.

Student loan
Want to go to university or college, but worry you might not have all the money to pay for it? You can take out student loans from a bank. A student loan is the ultimate in good debt because it makes your life better in the long term. Get a degree, and you'll probably get a well-paying job someday. The interest rates are usually lower than for other loans, too, so the money is cheaper to borrow. Just remember—a student loan is like any other loan. You will have to pay it back! Want to know more? Go to your local bank or talk to your parents or a teacher.

Trade
You do this at recess all the time, right? Trade is simply exchanging goods or services.

INDEX

For author videos, fun book extras, and to check out more great titles from the publisher of OWL Magazine, visit our website at **www.owlkidsbooks.com**.

CAMBOT-3000

POP

COM